STFU AND LISTEN

David Buyer

Copyright © 2021 David Buyer

All rights reserved.

ISBN: 978-1-7367118-0-4

DEDICATION

I want to dedicate this book to my daughter Rebecca and my son Zachary. They put up with me dragging them to the dojo at a young age and I hope they have learned a thing or two about life in general and of the martial Way. I hope you two teach your children all these things as well. I tried to teach you enough about life that you can be the best person you can be in your own life. Be there for each other because the only ones you can truly count on is blood. Always keep that alive because without that you have nothing. No matter what, be there for each other. Your brother or your sister may not always be right but they will always be your brother or sister. I love you two very very much and am so proud of you both.

To my Dad, rest in peace and I forgive you. It's taken a long time for me to be at ease with everything. I wish things had been different and I did a few things differently but the past is the past and I will always remember you being there for me.

To my Mom, I love you and thanks for always being there for me no matter what. I know I was hard to deal with but I appreciate everything you did for me in my life. Blood is forever.

CONTENTS

	ACHKNOWLEDGEMENTS	i
1	IS THIS MORE CRAP	1
2	GET OFF YOUR ASS	11
3	HYPER VIGILANCE AND ALWAYS ON	35
4	GET FOCUSED, QUICKLY	44
5	MIND LIKE WATER BUT BRING THE FIRE	53
6	TAKING DOWN GOLIATH	62
7	FIGHT LIKE A GIRL	69
8	BASIC TECHNIQUES	77
9	ADVANCED TECHNIQUES	99

ACKNOWLEDGMENTS

Thanks to my daughter Rebecca Buyer for helping with the chapter "Fight Like a Girl" and with photography.

Thanks to Jason "Deuce" Barber for helping with the pictures.

Thanks to Sensei Amine "Hawkeye" Khoury for helping with the pictures.

Big thanks to Sensei, Dr. Michael Downs, to letting me be who I am in the dojo without trying to contain me into only "one way". You saw my strengths and weaknesses and let me be who I am, even when I was a psychotic mess. You have always seemed to be able to put things into perspective for me and I know you have my back no matter what. I've grown more under your tutelage than I have under any one else bar none.

A huge thanks goes out to all my brothers in the Leathernecks MC. You have had my back over the years through a lot of really bad times. You've put up with all my crap and not once ever lost faith in me. I'd probably be in prison or dead if it weren't for all of you. UFW1UFWA no matter what. Much love and max respect to all my brothers for life. LFFL.

1 IS THIS MORE CRAP

So here it is. Another Martial Arts slash Self Defense slash, whatever you want to call it book. There are so many out there that I want to be up front about this and make you either want to buy my book right away or put it back on the shelf and save your money. Most people skim the first couple pages to see if it's worth it or not so I'll try my best here. The only reason why anyone should buy this book is because there is something different that sets this apart from every other martial arts book out there. And there are a lot of them. What would that be? It would have to be a different perspective from someone who looks at things a lot differently than most people. Something different. Something that will make you want to read more and not put the book down and come back months later or even never.

This book is a brutal look at what really happens when you get into a fight. Everything from life or death situations to a bar room brawl. But there are lots of things that happen before you actually throw punches or try to defend yourself. This book will take you on a journey of how you can change the way you view people and all the little things they do that usually goes unnoticed. It will change your perspective on what's really going on around you. It will open your eyes to a whole new dimension of looking at things. Once you actually see what's going on around you then that's where your real journey begins.

Can it be a little scary? Sure. Want to become the guy that locks every door and closes every curtain at night, has alarm systems, cameras, all kinds of weapons hidden all over the place and trusts only a handful of close friends? Want to be the guy that you never want to startle or sneak up behind (if you can) because he will put you on the ground so fast that you think you just time warped on to the ground? Want to be the guy that focuses his whole life on being aware of everything and has a plan to "take down" anyone in his immediate vision? Sure, read this whole book and make it your life. Is this a wise choice? Absolutely not. Hey wait a minute, you say? I thought you said you were going to try to convince us that this was a good book to buy. It is. You just don't want to make this book your life because the people that do make this stuff their life have paid a very high toll for it. How do I know? Yup, I am one. And making this book the way I lived my life is an understatement.

Let's get into the nitty gritty. A lot of books out there will only provide techniques for one type of situation. Like a full on assault where you need to put down or kill your attacker or a situation like someone harassing your girlfriend at the local bar. Two totally different situations requiring different methods for stopping it. And no, whoever tells you to eye gouge someone at a bar has NO clue about the law and the consequences of using those kinds of techniques in those situations. There are much more effective techniques which won't land you in prison that can stop an aggressor in his tracks.

Where is this book going to take you? For some, it's going to open your eyes and maybe change the way you train or give you more of an insight to how altercations happen. Or for others, it might really piss you off. Or for some, it will be a waste of money because you know everything because you're a genius. Some will take everything in this book and make it their life even though I warn against that several times in this book.

What do I say? I really don't care about someone getting pissed off from reading this book or thinking they know everything. I know what I write is the truth. Like it or not. This book is going to take you on a journey into the mind of someone who lives the life of always being "on". Yeah, the one I warned you about becoming if you took everything in this book and lived by it. What do I mean by "on"? Its name is hypervigilance. It's a state of awareness that makes you extremely sensitive to your surroundings. It feels like you're alert to any possible hidden dangers that can affect your life in a bad way. Often, though, these dangers are not real which is why this kind of behavior is classified as a mental disorder.

Everywhere you go you notice the people around you, the rooms or buildings you're in, the smells, the noises, the interactions between different entities, and everything else around you. Sometimes I call it my spider sense. It's a constant, always on scan and analysis that you can't turn off. Why? Because you made hypervigilance your life. A lot of military veterans are stuck in this state. It's not a good place to be because it takes its toll, but it is what it is, and you have to deal with it and not let it ruin your life. But one of the good things about it is that you DO notice everything and analyze everything. And believe me, I have been hypervigilant for the last thirty years or more now. I have paid a huge toll and have been through two marriages and numerous jobs because of it and am now on medications from the Veterans Administration Hospital (VA) not to mention counseling and psychiatric sessions from the same.

Once I started taking medications and counseling after thirty years of dealing with this, I started seeing that I wasn't the only one who was in this state. Like I said, a lot of vets are stuck in this state. I told myself that I wasn't going to try to change myself or hide and ignore it anymore as I had for so long. I was going to use it to help others. And this book came right to mind. Why? Because I realized that there was a whole new point of view about fighting. There's much more to it that just fighting. There are all sorts of things to learn before any fighting even has to happen. Yes, all the hypervigilance stuff. I also realized that I was doing these things on a daily basis without even actively knowing I was doing them. So I looked back at the things I did over the years and analyzed them all and tried to put them into something legible that anyone could follow.

If you've read this far you've probably bought the book so this is my way of giving back to you my knowledge so you can maybe better your life and help you or your family in an altercation down the line. Don't take this as a way to live your life. Take it as a way to LOVE your life and the people around you. Help others who don't have the means to help themselves and use this knowledge to make the world a better place for everyone.

Let me first start out with giving my background in order to fill in some blanks. Best way to do that is for me to take a seat on the couch and tell you all my dark secrets and what makes me, me.

Where do I start? It all started out way back in my childhood. My family moved to a town where most everyone had money. We didn't. We all know places like this. My parents moved there and as soon as I could remember, I knew I was different. My family didn't have money and in a town like that, everyone knew it. But they wanted us to have a good education, which we got, at a cost. What was that cost? Well, as you might guess, it was a constant barrage of bullying and me trying to evade my attackers on a daily basis. I was getting my ass beat all the time.

Me, my sister, and baby brother

I knew all the trails and hiding places in between school and my house. When I was in the open I would try to get through it as quickly as possible so I could disappear into the forest. Sometimes it worked and other times I didn't make it. The more I ran the more the bullies wanted to catch up with me. I felt a huge sigh of relief once I made it into the forest because I knew I could hide out there for as long as I needed. I set traps along the way in case anyone followed me and I dug out secret lairs to hide in. Sometimes I stayed in the forest from the time I got out of school until it got dark because I knew the bullies were riding up and down the roads I had to eventually cross.

I remember trying to convince my parents to let me take Judo classes that were being offered by the town but my Mother was a pacifist and didn't want me to get into any of that. I did get to study archery for many years but that was as close to combat arts as I was going to get until I joined the United States Marine Corps a couple years after high school.

After high school but before the Marine Corps, I got involved with a whole bunch of bad people. All kinds of illegal activities were the daily theme. Drug distribution, weapons distribution, explosives distribution, (I ain't gonna give details for obvious reasons) and all sorts of other crazy nonsense. I was definitely compensating for my lack of fighting knowledge by hanging out with these types of people. It felt good to be feared even though I still didn't know squat about how to defend myself. I'm not proud of any of it but it does give you a whole new view into that world and the people who live in it.

Along with all that activity came a ton of altercations with some really bad people. I was always pretty lucky when it came to getting busted by the law in that I really never got locked up. And no, I never snitched on anybody either. And for all the really bad stuff I never got busted for, I did get busted doing something really stupid that got me into the Marine Corps which changed my life forever.

Some of my friends and I stole a full keg of beer from an open door at the local fire department. It was just sitting there and all the patrons from the big party were in the big room having a good time. So we took it and threw it into my car. Instantly I had four or five cop cars flying into the parking lot. I decided that in my infinite wisdom and at the urging of my idiot friends, that we could outrun all the cop cars in my Plymouth Horizon hatchback. So I took off and sped all through town. I just couldn't lose my tail of cop cars. So I pulled into a parking lot and we all bailed out and ran like hell. I kept running until I realized that it was my car and I had to go back to it at some point. Well, I went back and was immediately swarmed by cops. They told me that I picked one hell of an event to steal a keg from. I asked what event it was and they told me it was the Chief of Police's retirement party. Damn near every cop in the area was attending it.

So for all that I got locked up but what saved me, since I already had a long history with the local cops, was that I was already talking to the Marine Corps recruiters at the time and was pondering whether or not to sign the contract to go in. I got the go to jail or go to the military deal. I said I was joining the Marine Corps and they said good enough and try to stay out of trouble until I went. I didn't but that's not the point. But I did sign that contract immediately.

I went into the Marine Corps and selected infantry. 0311 brothers HELL YEAH (You'll know what I'm talking about if you're a Marine). I was soon selected to go to the Navel Intelligence Training Center to get into the intelligence field because of my scores on the ASVAB. There I went through all sorts of training including intelligence, counter intelligence, surveillance, interrogation, and all sorts of other stuff.

IS THIS MORE CRAP

From there I was deployed to Okinawa to join the 3rd Surveillance, Reconnaissance, and Intelligence Company. One day a friend of mine told me about training in karate at the local gym on base. He said I should go and I did. That's where I met Sensei Eizo Shimabukuro. I trained with him for two years and shortly after starting training with him, I was asked to come to his home dojo. Only his top students were allowed to go there. He said I could kick like a horse and was constantly kicking other students into the wall. He also said I was a very aggressive fighter and tried to work around my style so that I would get the most out of his training.

It was a great introduction to the martial arts even if I didn't know who this man was at the time. I just thought he was another chicken farmer in Okinawa who just happened to know karate. It was only after the Marine Corps did I find out that he was the younger brother of Tatsuo Shimabuku, the founder of Isshinryu karate.

I was deployed to the Philippians several times and was charged with surveillance on certain trails and near strongholds of the NPA. The NPA were a terrorist group trying to overthrow the government. We were also charged with keeping an eye on the Philippine jungle intruders who were always trying to break onto the base and steal whatever they could.

This is where, among other places, that I really got to test out a lot of what I had learned. Let me say this. I am not proud of what I did out there. I was young and didn't really care about anyone or anything. We would go out on patrols and run into Filipinos who we questioned and if I didn't like the answers or they didn't want to come back to the base with us, I would beat them down. Badly. This also happened out in town on liberty as well. If I didn't like something someone said or did, I just went after them. I wanted to see if what I had learned actually worked. Some of it did and I paid attention to what did and what didn't. Unfortunately all at the expense of someone who probably didn't deserve the beat down.

Being a Marine, we also liked to fight anywhere and everywhere. And fight a lot. If we weren't fighting someone out on ops then we'd be fighting each other in the local bars on liberty. I have no idea how many fights I was in back then. One thing I did remember was what worked and what didn't. The techniques I used in the bars with other Marines, wasn't what I used in the field. I would have ended up in Leavenworth prison had I used some of the more vicious techniques. But they were not warranted. Every situation is different and one type of technique doesn't fit every situation. No matter what anyone says.

And no matter what anyone says, you will NOT win every fight nor will your techniques work out exactly like you practiced them in the dojo. Fighting for real is ugly and quick. I had my ass handed to me on numerous occasions. But fighting just because and fighting for survival or your family's survival are two different things.

During the Marine Corps I also trained in knife techniques, Muay Thai, and Arnis. I actually fought in Thailand at some bar with a Muay Thai ring. Most bars out there had them. We weren't supposed to fight in the ring but a lot of us did anyway. They offered me free beer and food if I got into the ring so I said sure. It took a little while to convince someone to fight me as none of the Thai fighters wanted to fight a karateka for some reason.

I want to tell you something about these Muay Thai fighters. These guys were about one hundred pounds soaking wet but when I hit them it felt like hitting a piece of iron. And they didn't even flinch when I hit them with all I had. I was all about power strikes and power kicks in my younger days. I immediately felt like I was in trouble and started to second guess my reasoning for even stepping into the ring. Oh yeah, free beer and food. I might get my ass beat badly but I'll have all the free beer and food I want. So I said to myself, ok, I just have to survive right now. So, at least when I was young, I was very quick on my feet so I just concentrated on going in quickly and getting out quickly and landing as many kicks and punches as I could because I knew a little bit about their point system and knew that they counted.

After the bell rang I was still standing but so was my opponent. He looked like I didn't hit him with anything at all and did absolutely no damage. I knew I had bruises all over my body but I didn't want to let on that I was hurting all over. Felt like I got hit by a bus. When the decision came in it was a draw, which I was more than happy with because at least I didn't get knocked out. I knew I didn't want to be one of those Marines I saw fighting earlier getting knocked out and then waking up asking what the hell just happened.

I remember my opponent coming up to me after and saying good fight and that I had one hell of a kick. I said it didn't look like I did any damage to you at all with my kicks but he said that it absolutely hurt him but that they were accustomed to not giving that away during a fight. Made sense but still scared the crap out of me during the fight.

Once I got out of the Marine Corps I got involved again, with some bad people. Yes, I should have learned my lesson but apparently not. Asset recovery jobs let me use my fighting skills without having anyone calling law enforcement on me (again, not going into detail here). I just told myself that these people knew what they were getting into and any consequences that happened were their own fault. Thankfully I didn't do that for too long and just started to concentrate on martial arts and doing as much as I could with that. Maybe it was me feeling bad for these people that taught me I had to learn more about martial arts. I had remembered all the things my Sensei had talked about in Okinawa. He was always so calm but could break a tree limb in half with his hand. And his yell could almost give you a heart attack. But he was the nicest guy I have ever met.

I remember sitting in front of a big bonsai tree in his yard for long periods of time in the traditional kneeling position. It looked out over the chicken farm and I could always hear the chickens. Could smell them too. But it was in front of that bonsai tree that I chose my place. A place that I would always remember how to relax and become still. Sensei Shimabukuro would always talk about how to relax. Breathe in and breathe out. He would tell us to picture in our heads whatever made you feel at peace. So I made the bonsai tree my place.

So once I started concentrating on martial arts, I studied more Karate, Muay Thai, Arnis, and the Karambit and picked up Aikido and Judo too.

I took along my two kids to as much of the training as I could. I do hope they remember those times like I do. It was great and I will always remember those times. They grow up so fast and I know they at least liked going to McDonalds after training and hanging out talking and eating. I loved doing that with them. I did use those times to try to teach them as much as I could about life and anything that came to mind. Don't really know if they listened or learned anything but hopefully they did.

Fast forward a number of years and it wasn't long before I had to use my fighting skills again when I got laid off from my last real office job. I decided to start my own home improvement company and quickly got work in Buffalo's west and east sides. Not very good neighborhoods as I had to be on my guard at all times. I could write a whole book on the stuff I saw and did down there. It was everyday ridiculous. It wasn't long before I didn't have any more patience with some of the degenerates I had to deal with. Mind you, this is all before I started talking to someone at the VA or taking my meds. I would actually look to get into something so I could kick the shit out of someone. I wasn't in the right frame of mind as I had already blown through my first marriage at this point. I had everything come at me down there including knife attacks, a gun pulled on me, baseball bat attacks, and every other form of altercation. I didn't carry any handguns at the time but I always had knives and batons. Sometimes I did pack a shotgun in my trunk, just in case. I also did evictions with the US Marshalls and most of the time I went in before the Marshall because I could fit through the window and he was confident in my abilities.

Funny thing happened one day though, after being pulled over for a traffic stop, I was arrested for having a baton on me. It's illegal to carry a baton here in New York as written in yet another one of their stupid restrictions. In handcuffs in the back of the squad car they asked me why I had it and I said that my K-Bar was in for repair and that I just grabbed the first thing I saw out the door. I told them what I did and what usually happened on a daily basis and you know what one of them said? He said, why don't you just get your concealed carry license and then you could shoot whoever came after me. I said to him, "So, you would rather me shoot someone who comes after me even if they're drunk and no problem for me to take down with less lethal methods?". Which was most of the time. I never got an answer but I did get let go because both of my brother in laws at the time from my second marriage were city cops and as a last resort I let their names fly before they decided to take me to jail. Thanks again guys.

So that story made me think. As I said in the beginning of this chapter, a lot of books have techniques that can kill someone and they don't talk about any of the consequences that will happen afterward. Especially if it's some drunk guy that only wants to be talkative and pushy. You don't take him down with lethal or guaranteed to be injured technique. You have to scale EVERYTHING to the situation at hand and you have to recognize what situation you're in IMMEDIATELY. That is the very thing that takes a lot of practice, especially if you're not one of the "lucky ones" who are always "on". And I say lucky ones with my tongue in my cheek. Trust me. I would love to NOT be one of the lucky ones but just a normal dude who likes to take martial arts and hasn't had all sorts of crazy issues over the years. I would have loved to be someone who was never divorced and had the nice house with the white picket fence around it in a nice neighborhood with nice neighbors and nice friends. I would have loved to be the person who didn't screw up half his life and that got help a long time ago to deal with all the bad stuff inside my head. And last but not least, I would love to just be normal.

Well, it is what it is for me and I just hope that out of all the darkness that I can actually help someone with this book. Shit happens in life and it's how you deal with the shit that matters. Even if it's long overdue.

Little word of advice from all this? Always remember that you can't un-see, un-hear, or un-do something once it happens. So be careful what you get yourself into in life and stay away from people who you know are going to bring you down. Even if you have the slightest doubt about them, get rid of them. It's not worth it to mess yourself up like I did.

I am going to try and have something in here for everyone. Not just the long time martial artists but for anyone not trained as well. The bad guys don't have a preference on who they attack and they have no idea if you know anything or not. Nor do they care either. Whether it be an armed robbery or a rape or just some asshole who thinks you looked at him wrong, none of these people give a crap who or what you are or know. Nothing about an altercation is fair or honorable no matter what type it is. Just keep that in mind as you read on and hopefully learn something along the way.

Now just sit back, grab a cool drink, and STFU and Listen.

2 GET OFF YOUR ASS

So I had a bunch of chapters written and I couldn't decide what to start off with. Then it came to me. In order to fight your way out of any situation you'll actually have to be somewhat active and fit. Wow, crazy concept right? You don't have to be a world class body builder or MMA cage fighter to fight successfully but you do have to have some degree of fitness. Let's be real, if you think you're going to be able to defeat an attacker who wants to hurt you badly, or worse, then you can't be some morbidly obese slug who will get winded going up a couple steps on a flight of stairs, or some skinny ass, bones sticking out, feather who folds in half after getting yelled at. If your one of those people reading this book then come on, get off your ass and do something about it. If not for you then maybe for your children. God forbid you have your kids with you when someone decides you and your kids are a good target. What are you going to be able to pull off if you're one of the above named useless human beings? Most likely you're not going to be able to do anything and have to watch your children get taken from you, beat to a pulp, or even murdered. And if you don't have children then just replace the word children with mother, father, brother, sister, niece, nephew, etc.

Well if that doesn't get you motivated to do something about your useless body and fitness level then I don't know what to tell you. At the very least do it for yourself and change from useless to useful. Do something, anything you can, but first you've got to GET OFF YOUR ASS.

Too many people put off getting in shape for a number of reasons. Again, you don't have to spend hours at the gym or exercising at your home if you don't like gyms. But you have to do something. Something to get you in better shape than you are now. Even if you're fit you have to keep it going because the older you get the harder it gets to stay that way.

I see way too many fat kids waddling around these days. And when you look at the parents they're duck waddling hippos as well. We as a society have to turn this around soon or we risk too many people dying because of obesity issues. And the more out of shape you are the more susceptible you are to not being able to fight off a virus or any number of diseases that are associated with obesity. We are way too politically correct when it comes to obesity. I don't care what you say about fat being ok. IT'S NOT OK. I'm not taking about a little fat because you don't have to be a body builder to be in shape but get real, get up and do something about it or there is a very good probability that you're going to die from something related to being overweight. Don't believe me then go ask your doctor for his HONEST opinion. If you have children then get them off their video games or whatever they're doing locked away in their bedrooms and get them outside. You as parents should be doing the same thing. Lead by example people.

When I was a kid my parents had to come get us when it was time to come in because we spent as much time as we possibly could outside. We played football, hockey, and all sorts of other stuff outside. We ran around, we climbed, and we were active. Getting grounded and having to spend time in our bedroom was actually a punishment and we did whatever we could to make our parents not mad at us so we could go back outside and play. I don't care if it was monsoon raining, we would still be outside playing in the mud. If we fell down we got back up. If we got scraped up we washed it off and went back out. Come to think of it we probably knew more about first aid than the kids do today but that's another story for a different book.

Anyway…… getting off my soapbox, let's get into it. Where do we start if you really want to get off your ass and do something? There is so much out there to choose from and not all of us have a ton of money to spend. Well, we have gym memberships, fad diets, personal trainers, and the list goes on and on. We spend billions of dollars each year in America on all these things looking for that perfect body and fitness level but we want it yesterday and not everyone is willing to do what it takes to get into shape. What if we didn't need ANY of those things? What if I told you they're all a useless waste of money? If your saying, "hey, I already have this stuff", don't worry, you can still use them as additional help, but just don't rely on them. You don't really need them. Plus, I bet most of the stuff you already bought is sitting around in your basement not being used anyway. That thousand dollar treadmill is probably a cloths rack right now. You should have saved your money.

So how are we going to get fit without all this stuff? What if all that we needed was ourselves? Nothing else. What am I talking about? I'm talking about your using your own body. Worried about being to light? Doesn't matter. Too heavy? Gotta start somewhere. Maybe putting down that 3rd cheeseburger might help right? This is straight up warrior training. It has been tested and proven over and over again thousands and thousands of times.

You're now asking, yeah right, where are the studies so I can go through them and fact check everything. Well, there aren't any. Even if there was, the health and fitness moguls wouldn't like them and would say no way, you need our products to get that kind of muscle. But I am saying that in no way shape or form do you need ANYTHING but yourself.

Well, what's the workout? How and where do I go to start? Well, there's a hard way and an easy way. The hard way would be to go and commit a violent felony and get caught. Make sure it's not the first time you commit a violent felony to make sure you actually go to prison.

I know everyone at this point is going "what the hell did he just say?" Read on.

So once in prison you can now begin. It's called the Prison Workout and every inmate in your prison will know what it is. All based on body weight exercise and isometric exercises.

Ok, now that I've said that, here comes the disclaimer. DO NOT go out and commit a violent felony. Hopefully you read this far and didn't drop the book to go do an armed robbery in a quest for the perfect body workout. You don't want to meet some of the guys you will meet in prison.

But those guys in lockdown can produce huge muscles in a relatively short amount of time and in their world, looking like you could snap someone in half is a necessity for surviving long prison stays. So the proof and studies on muscle building are locked up in prisons all across the world. Don't believe me? Go and ask any corrections officer about it. They can tell you. And if you do know someone who was locked up for a long time I bet they don't look like they did before they went in. Of course they will have the wear and tear from all the stress but they will have built up some decent muscle and fitness levels. Unless they ended up being someone's prison wife that is. So if you actually do go to prison concentrate on the Prison Workout as quickly as you can. Or start now before you go to prison so you don't become someone's prison wife.

Inmates all across the globe have access to the best fitness system in the world. It doesn't matter if they're locked up in solitary confinement 23 out of 24 hours a day. It doesn't matter if their food isn't prepared with their nutritional well being in mind. It doesn't even matter if they have anything at all at their disposal. It just doesn't matter. Make no mistake; these guys can put on muscle without any of those high cost items we are constantly encouraged to buy.

Prison workouts are all based on body weight. They also incorporate all kinds of different isometric exercises that you can do anywhere and some without anyone even knowing your doing them. The list and variations can go on forever. There are so many variations that even being used to the Marine Corps workouts I didn't know all of them. There are all kinds of things you can do so you don't get bored with the same thing over and over. But don't think because you do a few pushups every other day means that you're going to build anything other than sore arms. You need to commit to them and push beyond your limits.

Ok, so where do you start? Well, if you're really out of shape then you should probably go to your doctor and ask what you can and can't do right away. Matter of fact, everyone should consult a doctor before starting any workout. Get their clearance to start a workout. That's the first thing because if you're serious about getting in shape then I don't want anyone keeling over and dying on me. Take a highlighter and highlight the different exercises in this book and bring it to your doctor. He should be able to tell you with more detail what you can and can't do. Then listen to him and go home and GET OFF YOUR ASS.

Anyway, I could write a whole book on this stuff but that's not the intention of this book. I will however, tell you how to get started with a workout that should keep you busy long enough to then start adding and modifying the workout to your liking. Remember the first part of this workout is to get off your ass. After that it's up to you.

So here we go. Let's start with the hated pushup. Why do I say hated? Because every time we do them at the dojo I look around and see the looks on people faces. The "damn, I hate pushups" face. Well, they're very beneficial for your body. There are many variations of the push up but let's do the regular old push up for now. Make sure to go all the way down and all the way up. Keep your legs and body straight. Hands are shoulder width apart. Don't hold your breath but breathe out when going up and breathe in when going down. Do them as fast or slow as you want but make sure you pay very close attention to your form. No curved backs or pelvises hitting the ground or the funniest one, the head ups where you just move your head around to make it look like you're doing something. DO IT RIGHT OR DON'T DO IT AT ALL.

Make sure you can do at least ten of them before you move on to the next exercise.

Well, if pushups were first then what's usually next at the dojo? Yup, the sit-up. Yeah, I know, I see all the "I hate sit ups" faces out there too. So what's the correct way to do a normal sit-up? Sit down on the floor. Put your feet under something that will hold them down and keep your legs bent. If you can do a sit up without putting your feet under something then good for you. Lie back and put your back on the ground. Never let your head touch the ground though. I do not like the hands behind the neck because it can put a lot of strain on your neck. I keep my hands in front of me and in a fighting position. Sit all the way up and touch your hands to your knees without extending your arms. That's the sit up.

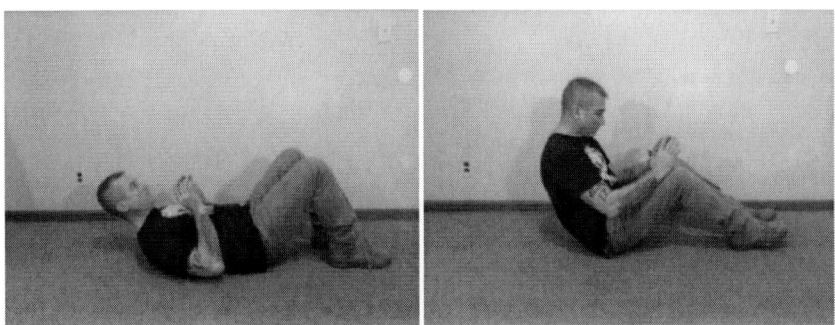

If you have had back surgery like me or have back issues then the crunch is a good alternative. The crunch is where you don't go all the way up but you leave your lower back on the ground and then raise your upper body and crunch everything together. You can really feel crunches in your abdominal muscles even more than the regular sit-up.

Before moving on to the next exercise make sure you can do at least ten sit ups.

Our next exercise is going to be burpees. In the military they were called Squat Thrusts. I start them standing up but you can also start in the up position of a pushup. To start, stand up and then squat down into a leapfrog type position and then from there shoot your legs back and out into the up position of a pushup. Then reverse it to go back up to a standing position. Very good for cardio.

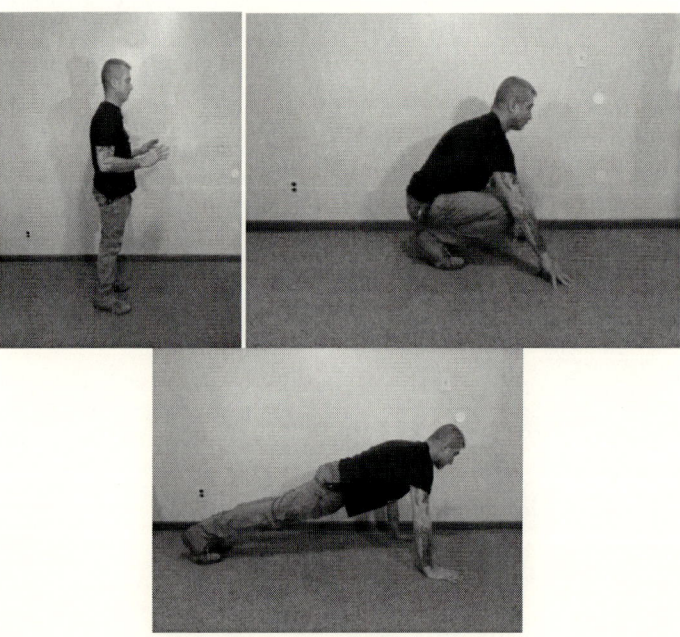

Make sure you can do ten of these before you go on to the next exercise.

Now that you're standing up already we can do the next exercise. It's the squat. Start in the standing position and then squat down as far as you can. The closer to the floor you get your ass the better. Do it slowly and make sure your back and head are straight. I keep my hands in front of me or on my waist because I don't like putting them behind my head and straining my neck. Make sure you're using proper form and if you feel pain in your knees then don't go down that far again. Work up to it and slow is the way to go.

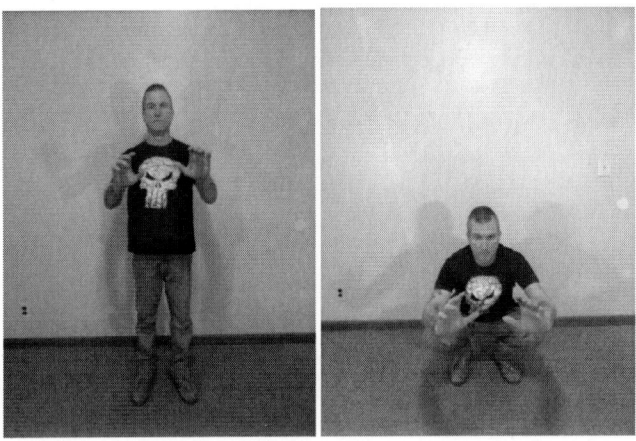

Make sure you can bang out ten before you move on.

This next exercise will burn your leg muscles really good. They're called stair climbers. So what you basically do is stand in front of a staircase. If you don't have any stairs then use something else. Big buckets, stacked tires, cinder blocks, I don't know, use your imagination. First, step up with the right foot and then follow with the left foot. Then step down in the reverse order. It doesn't matter which foot you lead with, it's all about the stepping up and down that matters. Two feet up and two feet down is one rep.

Make sure you can do ten and then move on.

Let's give everything a shakeup after doing all those exercises. The favorite of all exercises, jumping jacks. This is where everyone in the dojo goes YES, I can do jumping jacks easy. And then they do all sorts of lazy looking jumping jacks. Sometimes it looks like the floppy flipper convention came to the dojo. Again, do it right or don't do it at all. Make sure your feet go all the way out and your hands go all the way up. Clap your hands together at the top to make sure you get the best jumping jack you can. Or if you don't want to clap when no one else is clapping then just touch your fingers together at the top.

If you have shoulder problems like me then get your arms up as far as possible. Yes, I have a ton of injuries but I don't make excuses for them. I work through the pain and know where my limits are and train within them. Anyway, this exercise is about cardio.

Let's do jumping jacks until your heart is beating real good. I'll leave that up to you but try to push your limits. The Prison Workout is as much about cardio as it is about building muscles.

So those are the core exercises I use. If you were in the Marine Corps I know what you might be asking. Where are the pull-ups brother? Pull-ups are an excellent upper body workout. Trouble with them is that I wanted to lists exercises that can be done without any equipment. Like in PRISON remember? Sometimes I do them in my basement off the I-beam but you have to have really good finger strength to do a lot of them. Plus, you have to watch your head on the way up so it doesn't smack the beam. If you have a jungle gym in your back yard you can use that too. But again, I don't think they have jungle gyms in prison and if they do somewhere I hope if I ever get locked up that I go there.

Pull-ups are such a good exercise that I would recommend getting some sort of pull up bar for yourself. You know the ones. The ones that go in a doorway are just fine.

If you're just starting to get off your ass then work on these for awhile. Concentrate on these exercises before moving on to the isometrics. Do them throughout the day whenever you can. You don't have to do every exercise every time you have a moment but make sure you get them all in multiple times a day. The more the better. Just take things slowly and don't hurt yourself.

How many should you do before moving on to the isometrics? Here is your goal list:
Thirty or more pushups.
Twenty or more sit-ups.
Twenty or more burpees.
Twenty or more squats.

Twenty or more stair climbers.
Fifty or more jumping jacks.

Make sure you can do them all to the max. That means near perfect form and going to the fullest extent of range that you can do before you move on to isometrics. Make that heart pound and feel that muscle burn. You will start feeling a lot better once you start doing this every day. I promise.

Ok, you have met your goal and are able to do all the above listed exercises so let's move on to isometrics. What is an isometric exercise? They're contractions of a particular muscle or group of muscles and during the isometric exercise, the muscle doesn't noticeably change length and the affected joint doesn't move.

Ok great. You might be saying that you still don't understand. That's fine. Let's go into the exercises and you will see that the concept is real simple. I am going to list some of the isometrics that I like to do but there are literally hundreds of isometric exercises that are out there. The muscle groups that I am going to talk about are the shoulders, chest, back, arms, abs, ass, and legs. You might be saying that the neck is a good one too but a lot of the isometric exercises for the neck can damage the neck if you're not already fit. It's just too easy to damage your neck if you don't know what you're doing and I don't want to see anyone have to sit back on their ass if they hurt their neck.

If you're a doctor then you can probably name all sorts of other muscle groups and break everything down to a fine detail but I am focusing on those groups to get you either started or maintain your fitness level if you're already fit. After you see what they are I'm sure that you can come up with all sorts or variations.

One very important thing to remember about isometric exercises is to breathe while doing them. Also make sure that after you release from the isometrics that you do it slowly. This way you can prevent any injuries. Keep all that in mind when you start doing isometrics. Always

Let's start from the top down. The shoulders. There are a lot of different muscles in the shoulder so I am going to give a few examples that will hit different parts of the shoulder.

The first one, number one shoulder, you can use a towel if you're worried about scraping up your hand but I only use a towel if I'm rehabilitating a damaged knuckle. Stand facing a wall and bend your elbow at 90 degrees.

Make a fist and place your knuckles on the wall. Without moving your body, press into the wall with your fist and hold for ten seconds and then release slowly. Make sure you're breathing through the whole exercise. Do both sides and that will be one rep.

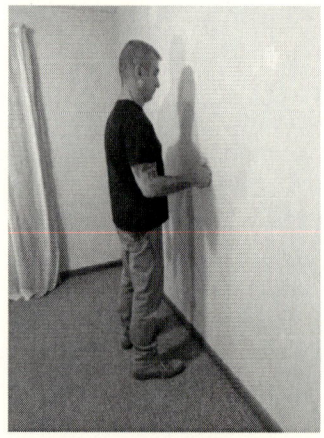

Do ten reps.

Number two shoulder exercise you will stand with your side about six inches from the wall. Your arm should be straight and hanging at your side. Make a fist and press it into the wall like you're trying to lift your arm up sideways. Hold for ten seconds and then release slowly. Make sure you're breathing through the whole exercise. Do both sides and that will be one rep.

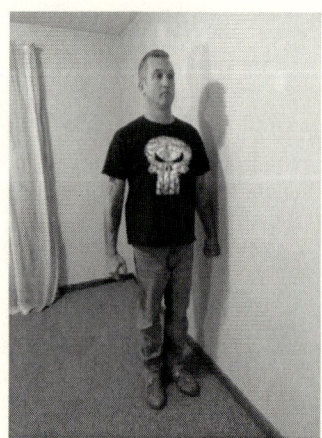

Do ten reps.

Number three shoulder exercise you will stand with your side about six inches from the wall. Bend your elbow at 90 degrees. Make a fist and press the back of your fist into the wall like you're trying to rotate your arm outwards. Hold for ten seconds and then release slowly. Make sure you're breathing through the whole exercise. Do both sides and that will be one rep.

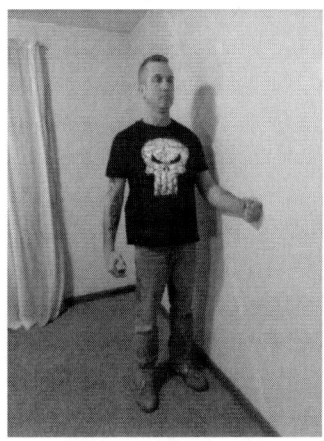

Do ten reps.

Number four shoulder exercise you will stand facing a corner wall. Bend your elbow at 90 degrees. Make a fist and press the inside of your fist into the corner wall like you're trying to rotate your arm inwards. Hold for ten seconds and then release slowly. Make sure you're breathing through the whole exercise. Do both sides and that will be one rep.

Do ten reps.

Number five shoulder exercise you will stand with your back about six inches from the wall. Your arm should be straight and hanging at your side. Make a fist and press the side of your fist into the wall like you're trying to push your arms out behind you. Hold for ten seconds and then release slowly. Make sure you're breathing through the whole exercise. Do both sides and that will be one rep.

Do ten reps.

Number six shoulder exercise you won't need a wall for. You will need a regular bath towel. Take the towel and hold it at each end. Extend your arms out in front of you and pull in opposite directions with your arms. Make sure you bend your elbows a little as you can put unnecessary strain on them. Hold for ten seconds and then release slowly. Now do the same thing but with your arms extended straight up in the air. After that, same thing but behind your back. Make sure you're breathing through the whole exercise. Doing all three positions will count as one rep.

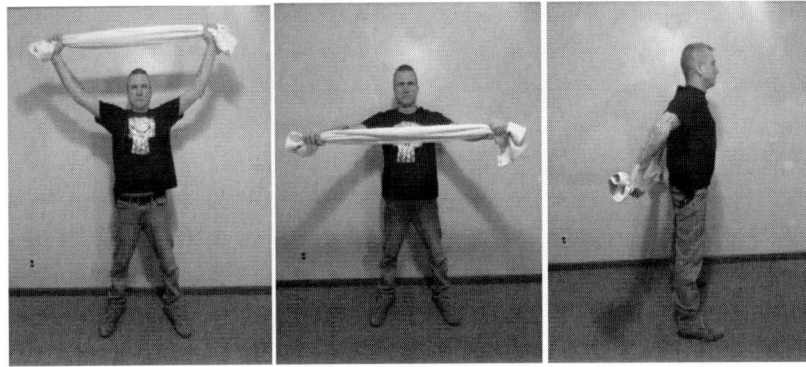

Do ten reps.

That's it for the shoulders. You should absolutely feel the burn after doing them all. Remember correct form and try not to move anything around. Your muscles should be flexed the whole time but as in the definition of isometric exercises, the muscle doesn't noticeably change length and the affected joint doesn't move. Kind of get it now? Not too difficult and you can do it anywhere.

Let's move on to the chest. Very important to develop good strong chest muscles because this is where someone hits when they miss other targets. I like to redirect any punches when they come in hard and if I don't move fast enough they usually run their fist into my chest. I'll take those hits any day over other places that would do more damage. If you like trapping techniques then this is where you would redirect any strikes into.

Number one chest exercise you will be standing up placing your hands in front of you in a praying fashion. Bend your elbows at 90 degrees and press your hands together while concentrating on your chest muscles. Hold for ten seconds and then release slowly. Make sure you're breathing through the whole exercise. This is one rep.

Do ten reps.

Number two chest exercise stand facing the wall and place your hands against the wall at shoulder height with your body leaning inward at a slight angle. Some of my readers might know this position well. If you don't then good. Keep it that way. Press into the wall while lowering you shoulders like you're trying to move the wall. Hold for ten seconds and then release slowly. Make sure you're breathing through the whole exercise. This is one rep.

Do ten reps.

Number three chest exercise stand inside of a doorway with your arms outstretched to the side at shoulder height. Now press your arms forward into the door frame like you're doing standard bench fly's. Hold for ten seconds and then release slowly. Make sure you're breathing through the whole exercise. This is one rep.

Do ten reps.

Now on to the back. Keep your back strong because that will help you with any injuries and recovery if you ever hurt your back. I have blown discs in my upper, middle, and lower back and have two surgeries under my wing. I still do as many back exercises as I can to keep it as strong as I can.

Number one back exercise you will put your hands on your hips. Gradually pull your shoulders back squeezing your upper back together. Hold for ten seconds and then release slowly. Make sure you're breathing through the whole exercise. This is one rep.

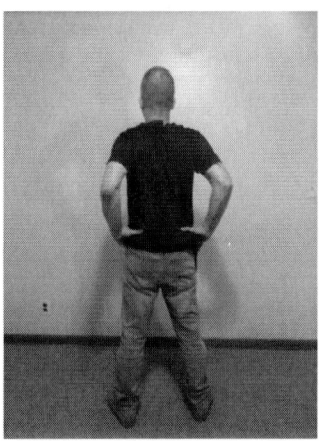

Do ten reps.

Number two back exercise you can be sitting down for. Make sure you're sitting up straight. Put your hands together in between your legs in a praying fashion with your fingers pointed down. Press your hands together and concentrate on flexing the lower outside of your back (latissimus dorsi). Hold for ten seconds and then release slowly. Make sure you're breathing through the whole exercise. This is one rep.

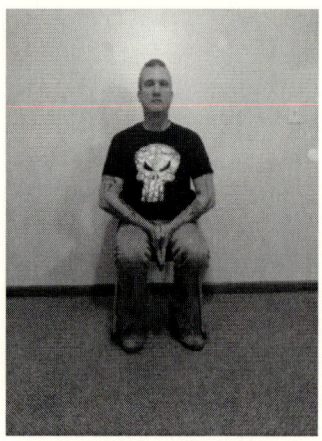

Do ten reps.

Number three back exercise you should recognize if you do any exercising at all. It's sort of like a reverse plank. Lie on your stomach and hold your arms out and elbows at 90 degrees. Your hands should be flat on the ground near your head. Lift your legs, upper body, and hands up as far as you can go. Hold for ten seconds and then release slowly. Make sure you're breathing through the whole exercise. This is one rep.

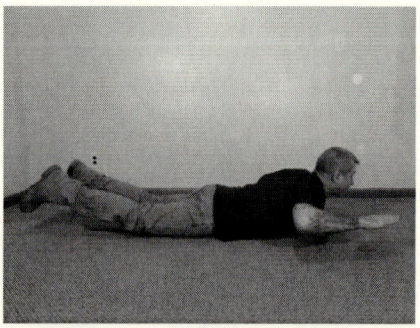

Do ten reps.

So now we get to everyone's favorite. The arms. Yeah, everyone loves big biceps because they're associated with being strong. Funny thing is that it's actually your triceps that are used while punching. The bigger the triceps the harder the punch can be. So let's get into the arms. These isometrics are good ones because you can do them just about anywhere and not look weird doing them. Make sure you breathe or it will look like you're trying to take a crap.

Number one arms exercise you will be sitting on a chair. Grasp the sides of the chair with both your hands. Keep your arms straight and bend your wrists a little. Now try to pull the chair up while still sitting on it. Hold for ten seconds and then release slowly. Make sure you're breathing through the whole exercise. This is one rep.

Do ten reps.

Number two arms exercise you will need an immovable object that you can sit or stand in front of. Like maybe your office desk or a fixed table. Bend your elbows at 90 degrees and put your hands face up under the object. Now lift up like you're doing a regular curl. Hold for ten seconds and then release slowly. Make sure you're breathing through the whole exercise. This is one rep.

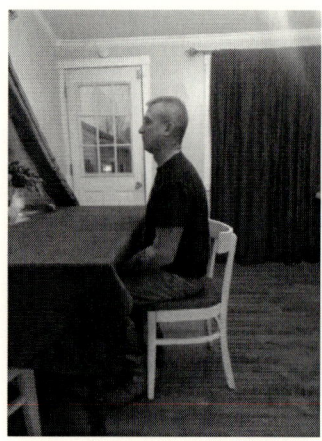

Do ten reps.

Number three exercise is just like a reverse dip if you know what that is. Use whatever you can find. A bed, table, couch, desk, or whatever works. It has to be solid though and not easily moved. Face the object with you back to it. Then with your arms at your side place you hands, with the fingers pointing down, on the edge of the object. Now lower your body down as far as you can go and then right back up. Once your arms are ALMOST locked out then lean back a little to put even more pressure on your triceps and hold. Hold for ten seconds and then release slowly. Make sure you're breathing through the whole exercise. This is one rep.

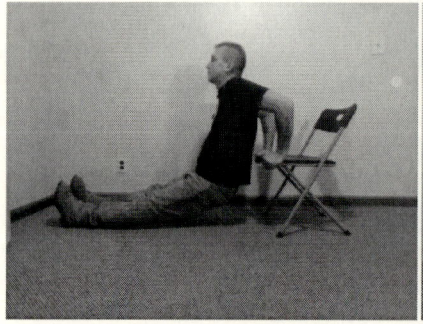 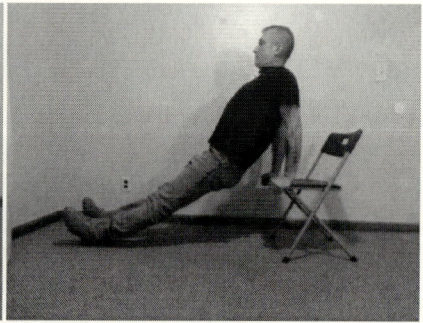

Do ten reps.

Another favorite among just about everyone is the abdominals. Everyone loves to have that "six pack" look. Here are some great isometrics for your abs. A lot of abs isometrics focus on breathing so it will help with your overall well being as well and tighten up those muscles. And strong abs make your back stronger as well.

Number one abs exercise you will be sitting up straight on a chair and take a deep breath in while paying close attention to flexing your abs. When you can't suck in any more air then slowly breathe out while still tensing up your abs. You will also want to raise your pelvis up and your ribcage inwards so as to really get your abs tighter. This should all take thirty seconds but if you can do it longer then great. The key is how slow you do it. This is one rep.

Do ten reps.

Number two abs exercise is a variation on the plank. Lie on the ground on your side with your elbow under your shoulder. Now lift you pelvis up while flexing all your abs and hold for thirty seconds. Then release slowly. Make sure you're breathing through the whole exercise. Now do the other side. This is one rep.

Do ten reps.

Number three exercise you will be lying on your back with your legs on a wall with an incline of about 45 degrees. Use your hands under your butt or use a pillow. Now breathe in and out and take as long as you can to do both while flexing your abs the whole time. Make sure you do everything slowly. This is one rep.

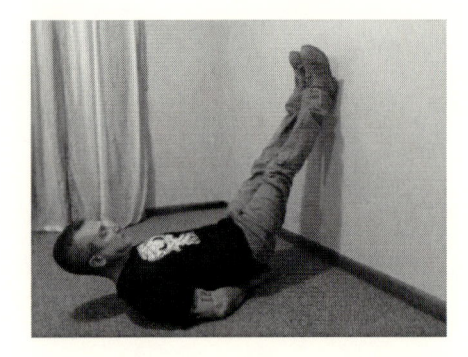

Do ten reps.

Now let's move on and tighten up that ass. Take some of that fat off your ass as that's where most fat goes and if you have no ass then put some muscle on it so that you can take a fall.

Number one ass exercise you can do anywhere. Sit down somewhere and the squeeze your butt together like you just realized you have to take a crap but waited too long to go. Hold for ten seconds and then release slowly. Make sure you're breathing through the whole exercise. This is one rep.

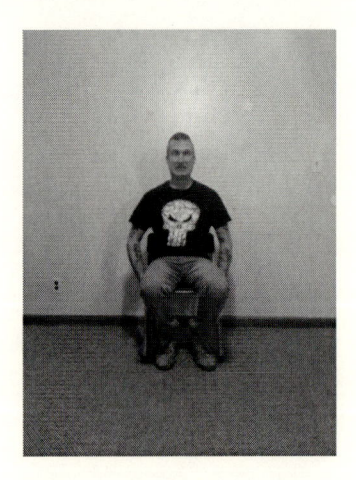

Do ten reps.

Number two ass exercise you will be on your hands and knees with your hands under your shoulders and knees under your hips. While still keeping your knee bent, raise your right leg up to hip level, hold for ten seconds, then lower it back down. Do the same with the other leg. Make sure you're breathing through the whole exercise. This is one rep.

Do ten reps.

Number three ass exercise you can stand behind a chair while holding onto the it with your two hands. Now raise your leg keeping straight behind you. Don't lean but raise the leg as far as it can go. Hold for ten seconds and then release slowly. Do the same with the other leg. Make sure you're breathing through the whole exercise. This is one rep.

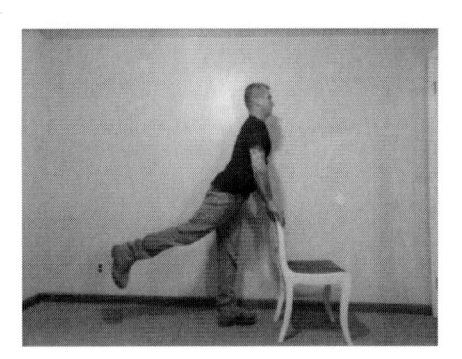

Do ten reps.

Number four ass exercise is the same as number three ass exercise but you lift your leg out to the side instead of back. Again, don't lean but raise the leg as far as it can go. Hold for ten seconds and then release slowly. Do the same with the other leg. Make sure you're breathing through the whole exercise. This is one rep.

Do ten reps.

Lastly, the legs. A lot of fitness nuts always seem to forget the legs for some reason. You see these guys all the time with huge upper bodies and the scrawny chicken legs. It's the weirdest thing. Its gotta be bad for their knees and legs joints as there isn't even enough muscle to hold up that big upper body.

I asked one of my sensei's a long time ago, while watching one of the strongest man contexts on TV, how in the heck do you take down a dude that big? I will talk about taking down big guys in another chapter but the first thing he said was "take out his knees". Then I looked at some of those guys legs and what do you know? Yeah, a lot of them didn't look like they paid any attention to their legs. So let's start building up those legs.

Number one leg exercise is one that I remember from Marine Corps boot camp. Yeah, I got in trouble a lot. With your back up against the wall slide down into a sitting position like you were sitting in a chair. Your knees should be at 90 degrees. Hold for ten seconds and then release slowly. Make sure you're breathing through the whole exercise. This is one rep. If you want to hold it longer you can.

Do ten reps.

Number two leg exercise you will go up on your tip toes. You can use a wall for balance if you like but make sure all the weight is on your legs. This is great for the calf muscles. Hold for ten seconds and then release slowly. Make sure you're breathing through the whole exercise. This is one rep.

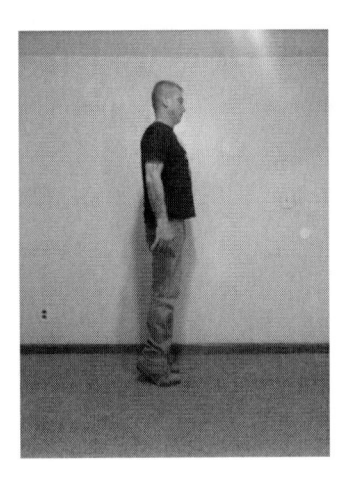

Do ten reps.

Number three leg exercise looks like a lunge but it's a little different. Go down into a lunge position. Your trailing leg is just for balance. Your front leg should now be flexed. Your knee should be at 90 degrees and your quad muscle parallel to the floor. Hold for ten seconds and then release slowly. Now do the other leg. Make sure you're breathing through the whole exercise. This is one rep.

Do ten reps.

So all of those were the basics you can take and get into some sort of shape. Remember, the goal of all this is to be able to defend yourself so don't get hung up if you don't look like you could compete in a body building contest. If that's your goal then you're going to have to do more research yourself and add stuff to your workout. Remember, this chapter was about the Prison Workout. Not a lot of stuff to work with in prison.

Don't forget to check out other resources online to find different variations on all the exercises in this chapter and also find new ones that you can put into your workout. There are so many exercises and iso's online that you could start tailoring your own workout and keep them interesting. You are your own trainer here and the sky's the limit. The main thing is that you don't need to spend a ton of money, or any money for that matter, to get into shape. So if you have read this far without actually doing any of the exercises yet, then GET OFF YOUR ASS and get started.

3 HYPERVIGILANCE AND ALWAYS ON

I know you hear some people say to be more vigilant and pay attention to your surroundings. This is good advice but when, where, and for how long are you supposed to be aware? Ask different people and get different answers. Some say that they really don't pay attention until something happens and others are aware of everything and everybody that is anywhere in their view or anything that could possibly happen wherever they go. The first one is useless cause if you get attacked you will probably die a vicious horrible death. The later is a thing called hypervigilance and being always on, which is at the top of the proverbial awareness tree.

So where do you want to be? If you're the one that only looks up when you hear something out of the ordinary then you need to do a way better job at being aware. Because you're absolutely, not aware. This is not a good state to be in and I call it, being "always off". Forget about someone attacking you, you have a good chance of getting hit by a car while crossing the street. Put away the damn phone and pay attention dumbass. I see these idiots crossing the street and not even looking up, like they're trying to prove that they can walk across the street without looking and everyone else has to look out for them. While they do technically have the right of way, what good is it and what are they proving by taking the chance on being smashed into a few different body parts. What if that driver was on his phone too? No, he shouldn't be, but you know they're out there. You will LOSE the battle of thinking you can take on a three thousand pound speeding car head on every time. If you think you can win that battle then you're a moron. And please make sure if you have kids to let them walk behind you and not next to you because sooner or later you're going to get hit by a bus.

HYPERVIGILANCE AND ALWAYS ON

Well after that guy we have the hypervigilant/always on guy. This guy doesn't miss much and what he does miss wasn't a threat to him anyway. You're thinking that this is the guy you want to be so there is very little chance that you will ever be taken by surprise and if you see something wrong you will be able to handle yourself? The problem with this guy is that there is a huge toll taken on him whether you think so or not. I have been, unfortunately, in this state for over 30 years. Probably longer, as I really can't remember back when I was younger but I probably was. The Marine Corps just sent it into overdrive. Anyway, I thought I was the only one like this for a long time until I sought the help of counseling services offered at the VA. I found out that I wasn't the only one and that I wasn't some kind of freak who had all these preparations and nuances every time I went somewhere. Even in my own house I was hypervigilant. Do you need to be like this to not get surprise attacked? Maybe no. Maybe yes. Maybe it's probably somewhere in the middle that is good enough and that won't cost you your mind.

What you need to be is hypervigilant when in spaces where you don't know everyone. Parking lots, hotels, bars, malls, stores, anywhere there is people you don't know and they can get to you easily. Even when you're in your car stopped at a traffic signal. Why you say? It's called a transitional space and that space, if the timing is right, is the perfect place to hit someone, probably rob or kill them, and most likely get away with it. You say, hey, I locked my car doors when I left home. Sure but you had your window down because you were NOT AWARE that you had left it open the day before. I'm sure with that in your head you can now probably think of many more spaces that you need to be more aware in.

Take the time to open your eyes and start looking for these spaces. You will be surprised how many of them you go through each and every day. Look around and see who's around you at any given time.

Here goes the training on being more aware.

As you get used to finding transitional spaces start checking out the people in them. There's a whole profession built upon analyzing people. It's called behavior analysis. The FBI uses these guys to solve crimes. Yes for real, not just on TV. But short of becoming a Federal Agent, what can you look for? Well let's take the most obvious first. The first thing that I usually take notice of is a person's eyes. That will then tell me if I have to look at them a little harder. Mind you, I am scanning all the time and it never really shuts off. It takes me about two seconds to determine whether a person is a threat or not and what they have on them if they are. Do you need to be

THAT aware? Well, that depends on where you go or if there is a need to do so. I'll be talking about situational awareness in a few.

What do I look for in the eyes? Let me say first off that you could write a whole book on this stuff so I will try to explain how I do it in a most general way. You should get the hint and then if you decide to take it farther then pick up some body language or behavior books and explore away. Be aware though that your spouse or girlfriend/boyfriend might not appreciate being analyzed by you. Cause I know that's what you were just thinking and I'm warning you ahead of time. I know this by experience. Believe me, sometimes I get caught doing this without even realizing I am doing it. That's the problem with always being aware/on.

So getting back to the eyes after that sort of disclaimer. I check out the person's eyes to check their mood. Are they wide open, partially closed, squinting, dilated, not dilated, shell shocked, intense, thousand yard stare, and ton of other things to look for? Each of these will tell me if I have to check them out more.

If I do think I have to check deeper, I check their facial expression and what their body is doing. You know that diagram at the doctor's office that tells your doctor how much pain you're in by the facial expression on the chart? It's sorta like that. Are they angry, sad, fidgety, twitchy, aloof, or a hundred other things? You have to make a split second judgment on the person's demeanor and assess whether or not to check them out even more.

Any of the ones that I deem a threat I roll into my third scan which is what they could be doing, what they have, and what they're going to do it with it. What kind of threat are they? Just someone that wants to be a pain in the ass or someone who wants to hurt someone. Where are their hands? Where are they looking? Who are they looking at? What direction are they going and what could be their destination? What is their MISSION?

This all needs to happen in a matter of seconds especially if there are multiple people around you like if you're boxed in while in a grocery store line. Once you're aware of one person who might be a threat is there anyone else that they're with that could be their accomplice? Scan, scan, scan.

Yup, this is the kind of thinking I unfortunately do on a daily basis. Yes, it's what I'm telling you to get better at but don't let it take over your life like it did mine. Be careful how you go about this and just practice it to the point where you can at least turn it off when you need to. If you really want to dive into this then there is a ton of information out there as far as body language, human behavior, micro expressions, and a whole host of different topics. They're pretty addictive once you start researching them but remember, don't let it take over your life. Gotta be able to turn it OFF.

And being able to turn it off and back on when needed is called situational awareness. This is the appropriate amount of awareness for the space that you're in. Awareness will be different when you're sitting in your garage having some beers with a bunch of your friends than in a bar where there are a whole bunch of loud mouth drunks. A big event that could be targeted by terrorists is a different situation than sitting at home watching the same event on your TV. It's all going to depend on the situation. And all situations are different.

Here is a truth that not a lot of people like to hear. Even with the best scanning in the world, you can cut down a lot of the chances for being taken by surprise but it's not foolproof. The crazy guy with a machete scenario? Yeah sure, if you were paying attention you would probably be able to see that guy coming but what about the guy in the trunk of his car snipping with his long range rifle? Or how about the terrorist that drives his truck through a large crowd? After its underway you might have a chance but what if you're the first one in line? Well then guess what? You're now KIA. That's dead if you didn't know. That's the cold hard truth.

If you're unfortunate enough to be the first victim in a surprise attack then there is usually nothing you can do and your time is up. Hopefully they didn't nail you with a head shot or hit you dead-on with the truck and you still have a chance if someone gets you to the emergency room quick enough to live but in those situations don't expect anyone to help you until long after everything is over. Which most of the time, for the first victims, is too long of a wait. You're dead. Sorry but it is what it is.

So maybe you're saying right now, what the hell, you don't have any advice for that? As a matter of fact I do. This is my advice. Make absolutely sure that you tell your loved ones EVERYDAY that you love them because you never know when you're time will be up. Be at peace with who you are and with whatever maker you believe in. Try to have your life in a relatively good place. Yeah I know. That one's a tough one for a lot of us including myself but I am trying everyday to make it better and help as many people as I can before my time is up. Since splitting up with the mother of my two kids ten years ago, I have talked to or hung out with my two kids just about every single day and each time I do, I always tell them that I love them.

Whenever they call I answer no matter what. Don't care if I'm with someone or doing something important. My kids are more important than anything on this planet and I will always be there for them. So if you have kids, do the same for them.

So that's my advice. Take it or leave it.

So getting back to our training, after scanning and finding the people who could possibly be a threat what can you do to prepare even if you don't carry a weapon or forgot to bring it. Because if you already have a weapon on you then use it right? Here's a good drill to get you into the mindset of being aware/on.

I was at a hotel getting a bucket of ice. I thought to myself as I was walking back to the room how many weapons could I count on me. This is what I had with me. My sandals, my shorts, my ice bucket, and the ice in the bucket. I didn't even have my room key on me. I know the people who know me are going, damn Dave, not even a knife? I was trying to teach myself how to turn things off ok? And no, I still haven't been able to accomplish that yet. So no weapons on me in that situation but did I have no weapons at all?

In the movies the person walking down the lonely hotel hallway would be the first one to die in a horror movie and seems the least prepared. But if you really look at it there are several weapons you can use. Now, forget about your fists or knees or anything on your body because we all know you can use those. But what if you're not a martial artist and don't really know how to defend yourself with your built in weapons? Well go join a dojo and learn right? Yeah probably, but maybe you just started going to the dojo and get attacked 3 weeks into your training. Forget about the mindset needed to actually defeat an attacker as I go over that in another chapter, but let's look at what we have to work with immediately. Let's start at the bottom up. My sandals. What can you do with a pair of rubber sandals? Well for one they leave a hell of a mark when you slap someone upside the head with them. Especially if they're wet. Don't forget about using them as a projectile as well. No, it's not going to take someone down by just hurling a sandal at them but they will probably put their hands up and pause for a second or so. Enough time to put some distance between you and them. Or, if you can't run, to make a valiant effort to punch them in the nose or kick them in the privates. So hitting someone with a sandal is not cool enough for you? Get over it. Fighting and defending yourself is NOT pretty. It's NOT like the movies. It IS fast and ugly. It's about getting out of the situation as fast as possible and continuing your life with your family and friends. That's it. Even if you're a black belt in whatever, it's still not going to be pretty. I don't care what anyone tells you, it's gonna be ugly.

Most of the stuff I do is quick, aggressive, and in your face techniques. I have taken all the arts I have learned over the years and made them my own. I use what has worked for me and I at least know about what doesn't. The more you know the more you can defend against. Not every technique will work for you depending on your psychical limitations or injuries or maybe you just don't like them. It doesn't matter. Whatever works then use it and own it. When someone asks me what style I train in I tell them I call it UglyDo or The Way of the Ugly. But it's what will get you out of almost every situation. Quickly.

So going back to the hotel, how about my bucket of ice? We already used the sandals as a projectile so why not ice and a bucket? Throwing ice cubes might seem desperate but hey, why not? The bucket can actually do some damage if you use it to swing or thrust into them. Good bonking device right?

The plastic bag in the bucket was really thin and seemed like it was useless. But then I thought why not use it if I had a chance to get a good choke on someone. I could use the plastic to put in my palm and cover their mouth and nose with it while I was choking them with one of my favorite chokes. One caveat though, watch out for their teeth. If you're good at chokes then it still takes a few seconds to put someone out. They aren't going to go down without a fight. So they might try to take a bite out of your hand or arm if given the opportunity.

And then, last but not least, my shorts. Well, if you're worried about taking them off because of modesty, then all I have to say is, better to expose yourself then be dead right? And if you take them off and start yelling like a crazy person you might just make the attacker leave cause who really wants to tackle a naked guy right? And again, the shorts could be used for a projectile, whip, or strangulation device.

I always laugh when I see the naked guy running out onto a sports field and the security guys chasing him. I'm wondering what is going through their minds as they're chasing him down. They gotta be like damn, I don't get paid enough for this shit. I gotta tackle this naked guy who's probably going to be flailing all over the place once we catch him. I'm pretty sure they let him run for as long as they can so he's all worn out by the time they catch him. It makes me laugh every time.

Anyway, flailing around and screaming at the top of your lungs like a psycho is what you need to do. Most attackers don't want that kind of attention. If it looks like you're going to be a problem for them then they will most likely take off. Don't count on it all the time but just be aware of it. Also don't count on anyone coming to help you cause they won't. Not until you're already beaten to a pulp lying on the ground and the attackers all gone. That's just the way it is so be prepared beforehand for anything. You should have done the scanning and situational awareness thing already and then maybe you don't get attacked in the first place right?

I hate the saying "thinking outside the box", but that's basically what you have to do to see improvised weaponry. You can't just think of something for its normal use. You have to open your mind and think. And think quickly if you're attacked.

So use scenarios and try to think of everything that can be used as a weapon and how to use it. Maybe make it a game for your family when out and about. You know, like the game "I Spy" that everyone plays on road trips. Probably call this one I Spy – Dark Version.

Call out "I Spy – Dark Version" at a random place and have everyone start naming all the weapons they see or are on them and what they can do with them. Like, I Spy a hand sized rock that I can throw, scrape, or bash someone in the head or face with or throw through the windshield of a passing car to get their attention and help you out or at least make the attacker run away. Yeah I know, now you gotta deal with a pissed of passerby that you just chucked a rock through his window but that's probably better than what the actual attacker had in mind for you. Then move on to the next family member. I Spy an iron rebar lying on the side of the road that I can throw, stab, beat and all sorts of other stuff with. I Spy a plastic cup that I can throw, jamb in the face, ears, throat, or other vulnerable areas with or rip it apart and use it as a cutting device. The more creative you get the better. Open your mind up and talk about all the weapons afterwards or during. Make it fun and everyone should remember it for a long time and maybe save one of your family's life someday.

Remember, the time to think about what weapons are available isn't when you're being attacked but way before that even happens. If you are accustomed to thinking about this all the time and just something you always do then when the time comes you will already be in the right state of mind to see what's around you and how to use them.

So hope I didn't ruin your favorite road game by releasing this dark version of it but it has to be done. You have to prepare your loved ones because one day they might have to protect you or their family. Give them the tools to do so.

Here is another way to get accustomed to paying attention to everything around you. Some of you will say it's too dangerous but if you want to be able to walk into any environment and look like you belong there then do this. Because looking like you're NOT a target is what we need to be. No victims.

So, if you live in a nice town with virtually no crime and cops that come to every call within minutes then you probably don't have to worry about running into bad situations on a daily basis and maybe you won't have to worry about it ever. Not everybody gets into altercations throughout their life. You can go your whole life and never see any conflict. Good for you. If that's you then that's a good thing right? Well what about that time you go on a road trip and get lost and happen to wander into some really bad neighborhood? The first thing that needs to be done is to not look like you don't belong there. Even if they know you're not from around there then have the bearing and posture to look like you do belong there. Have some intensity in your eyes and walk. You don't want to look like a target.

Go find a really shitty neighborhood and go to some corner store there. Yes, this is the start of the exercise. Walk in and go to the back to grab something off the shelf and go buy it. Walk in like you own the place and pay attention to your posture and intensity. Don't be an asshole but make sure you're scanning everything and everyone. Know where everyone is in that store and outside the door. Especially at the entrance. If someone says hi or talks to you then say hi and talk to them. Don't linger but make everything to the point. Don't pull out a ton of money but have a couple bucks in your pocket. Go outside and eat whatever you bought in front of the store or next to your car. Have an escape plan and use it if you're getting weird vibes about the people around you. You will have to remain calm at all times to get the most out of scanning at this point. Being scared is not good for paying attention to the things around you. If you're scared and let it take over your senses you will lose over half the information you would be able to take in if you had had control over your emotions. Why do you think when police question someone who just had something happen to them they usually say that they don't remember most of it and it happened so fast. That's because they lost control of their emotions.

So yeah, this exercise can go sideways real quick but if you want to train real world, then you need to place yourself into situations that you wouldn't normally be in. Why? Because you can't predict where something bad might or might not happen and you can't always be in a safe place for your whole life. Unless you're a hermit.

So, what if you're from that shitty neighborhood and reading this book? What can you do? I'm pretty sure if you live in those shitty neighborhoods then you probably have some kind of awareness going on anyhow but I have seen a bunch of people in shitty neighborhoods that have no awareness whatsoever too. Well you can do the same thing but in a good neighborhood. What, you don't think people in nice neighborhoods don't know when someone doesn't belong there just like they do in bad neighborhoods? Well they notice there too. Just as much or maybe even more. Walk in like you own the place and carry yourself properly. Don't be an asshole if someone stares at you and say hi and talk to anyone who talks to you. Same thing as before just a different place.

Everything comes down to looking like you belong there and having some sort of intensity with you wherever you go. You have to always think like you're not a target. Most of the time I do this too much and I have gotten into arguments over the years about it. It's became a part of me that I can't turn off anymore. I've walked into places and saw someone I knew and then the people they were talking to said oh good, you know him? I thought he was coming in here to kill us. I've also gotten yelled at walking into my own bedroom when the door was shut. I would open the door real fast and walk in as if I'm doing a room clear military style. I usually get the "what the hell is wrong with you today"? So be careful and like I said before, don't get so far into it that you can no longer turn it off when you need to. A place in the middle is the way to go as we said in the beginning of this chapter.

So the first thing to work on is actually being aware. Even a little more is better than nothing. I promise you that if you start paying attention to the things around you then you will finally start to see the world as it really is and what's happening in it. It's a beautiful place and there is a lot of good in this world but there is also unfortunately, a lot of evil. Peace is great but in order for everyone to be safe and at peace then more people have to be aware of everything around them. Don't give a would-be attacker the chance to surprise you and become just another statistic. Take responsibly for everything you do and see. Once you have awakened yourself and are aware then you can start to see the things around you that could possibly hurt you and avoid them. Then turn it off when you get home. You might see a lot more of everything that doesn't hurt you as well along the way. There's a lot we miss by not being aware. You just have to open your eyes.

4 GET FOCUSED QUICKLY

If you've been training a long time or you've just started you know that there are days that you go in to train and the first thing that hits your mind is anything other than what you're supposed to be focused on. Maybe you're thinking about going home and eating that spaghetti dinner that you know is waiting for you, or maybe it's some crap at work, or maybe it's some stupid argument you just got into with your wife. I don't know but whatever it is it's not something you should be focused on when training right?

We all have these days. Sometimes it's like a funk that lasts a week or two or sometimes it's just a bad day. Whatever it is, we need to snap out of it if you want to get past that proverbial wall right?

Well the name of this chapter is GET FOCUSED QUICKLY and what I am about to say will do just that. And it will do it quickly. I know some people might not like what I have to say but I know for sure that it works because I use it. If I haven't done it, seen it, experienced it, or lived it I'm not writing about it. PERIOD.

What will get you focused quickly? Well, I don't always train like this but that's because not too many people even like to think about it let alone actually train this way. What I'm talking about is using live weapons. What do I mean by live weapons? A real sharpened knife, a real handgun, a real shotgun, a real baseball bat, a real bar stool, etc. I know what some of you are already thinking. This guy is just plain nuts. Well maybe, but this is what you will get out of using live weapons. You will get very VERY focused on the training you're doing when working with live weapons, especially sharp blades. You will develop a real respect for all weapons if you train with them in this way. Yes, you have to be very careful especially if training with a partner. And if you use firearms I don't recommend actually using live rounds unless you're at a special facility that can handle live rounds. This would mostly be for law enforcement and military but you could actually set something up if you had a lot of land.

Does anyone actually use live weapons when they train? Yes, we did this in the Marine Corps all the time. Do you think we went out there with wooden rifles or wooden bayonets? Hell no. We actually loaded them up with blanks or live ammo depending on what we were training for. Hey, you're going to have to use the real thing if you get attacked so why not train with what you will use?

Go very slowly at first and gradually build it up. Will you get cut if you're using a live blade? Probably. I have several scars from this kind of training. I just say they give me character. If you don't want to go the full live weapons training you can always use look alike or a real one modified. Why would I tell you to use a look alike or real one modified if I've just talked about using real ones? Because sometimes you have to do what you have to do to get started or not freak the hell out of your dojo partner that they don't ever want to train with you again. We don't want that to happen right?

What's a look alike look like? Well it's not one of those wooden knife or guns for sure. I'm sure you know of them if you go to a dojo. They're ridiculous and I don't use them. EVER. You train with that all the time and I guarantee you will never be prepared for the real thing if it does happen to you. Why? Because you will have never made the jump from playtime to staring down the barrel of a real gun or having a real sharp shiny blade glistening in front of you.

If you don't have a real gun to use then you can get the hard plastic formed training guns. They actually look exactly like the real ones but they're blue or whatever color you get them in. What I like to do is bore a hole in the barrel so it actually looks more like a real one and then paint it flat black. Yes, I know there have been instances of cops thinking one of these is real and shooting first, but you aren't going to use your bored out and painted training gun in a robbery right? If you are then put down my book and go away. Get real but don't get stupid. Got it?

Another excellent gun to train with is the blank gun. These actually fire blank rounds and look and function exactly like the real thing. You can get them in just about any handgun you can find out there. Really good for training because you can actually practice racking the gun after you do your take away techniques. And always remember to rack your gun after you take it away from someone. More on that in the Advanced Techniques chapter.

You can also get real looking blades as well but to take it even further, I took an old kitchen knife and grinded down the blade so it wouldn't actually cut someone. It was a real kitchen knife, like the one in the movie Psycho, but it was not going to do any damage to anyone. I even rounded off the point so it wouldn't hurt anyone. Believe me, I get the same reaction when I pull this one out unexpectedly as opposed to a real blade. You will get the deer in the headlights for a couple seconds. Just enough time for me to stab them several times before they realize what's going on. Not good right? And that's my point. You will never be prepared for the real thing if you don't train like this at some point.

And I'm not saying that if you train with live weapons that you will be prepared for the real thing because there are all sorts of other factors when the shit hits the fan but you will at least be more prepared than someone who doesn't train with live weapons. Guaranteed.

A problem I have when I bring something like the kitchen knife out is that most guys at the dojo will ask me to put it away. They say it's too dangerous. Hmm, a real kitchen knife grinded down so it's completely dull? I wonder what they do when they go home and their wife tells them to cut up all the meat for dinner. Maybe they get out a wooden training knife, that I might add doesn't look anything like a real knife to begin with.

Maybe that's why most people who train with the wooden stuff don't have any intensity when they do their disarm techniques. There is nothing that is actually getting them in that kill or be killed mode. You train like that and I guarantee you will freeze if it comes down to a real attack. And I also guarantee that if you actually train with a real weapon that you will immediately get focused real fast. Because the other option to not getting focused while using live weapons is getting cut, bruised, broken, hurt, etc. Get the point? No pun intended. Hey, when you train in the martial arts you're actually training to defend yourself and possibly take someone's life if necessary or hurt them so badly that they won't be a threat to you or your family anymore. There's the cold hard truth for you.

Wooden vs. Real

That's said, I have also seen blades with electrical shocking mechanisms in them. That's fine but I would also like to see something that actually looks like a knife and will shock the hell out of someone too. Maybe someone can invent one and let me try it out. My main point is that you have to give a person a reason to get the hell out of the way quickly. People get lazy in the dojo sometimes but if they get the snot shocked out of them with an electrical shock knife I will guarantee that the look on their face will change the next time you try to attack them with it.

Do I recommend that the first time you train with a live weapon that you pull out a sharpened blade and go balls out and start out flying all over the place? Absolutely not. You have to work up to a speed that you and your partner are good with. You also want to make sure that you have room because you don't want a live blade getting knocked out of your opponents hand and flying across the dojo and inserting itself into the nice $500 mats or worse yet, into someone's back. I think the owner might not like that and you might not be able to train there anymore. People tend to not like getting stabbed for real when training at their dojo.

I usually train alone or with one other person either outside or in a big room with only us in it. Less likely to have collateral damage. And if you're outside, be prepared depending on where you live to have to speak to the police about what exactly you're doing. I had the police stop by when I was practicing with big huge Rambo type blades in my back yard. Guess they got a report about some lunatic running through the backyard waving around a bunch of knives. Think they thought it was a domestic or something. Took a little bit of explaining especially when they showed up and I still had the blades in my hand. Next time I did that I put out a bunch of my martial arts stuff out so they could see that I wasn't a lunatic (maybe) but a martial artist.

So how do you go about starting up something like this? The best way is to build up to it. Do it by yourself for starters. I always say train with what you're actually going to carry. So if you like a certain fixed blade then get the closest training blade that resembles your real blade. Wait, did I just say training blade? Yes. If you're new to live weapon training you can't just go out, buy the sharpest blade you can find, and start whipping it all over the place.

Here's a good starter. I used to do this all the time. It's the butterfly knife. Even if that's not what you carry it's a good introduction into training with live blades. I had a ton of them confiscated by the police in my younger days. I always had one on me and I would flip it around all the time. Anyway, get yourself a nice training butterfly knife and an equivalent looking real one. I'm not going to list the exercises in this book as they're all over the internet. Just start practicing the techniques that they have online with your practice blade.

Once you have a couple good spins and techniques down then switch to the live blade. Try not to think about the blade because then you will get cut. Think of it as an extension of your hand. And if you really got those spins and techniques down pat with the training blade, you shouldn't have a problem doing them with a live blade. You just have to keep your mind focused and not let fear creep in. Do not let that happen. Focus.

One caveat I want to add. Getting good at tricks with a butterfly knife is pretty cool but I wouldn't recommend using that in any type of real altercation. It's just a good exercise to get you used to using a live blade and getting your hand-eye coordination up to speed.

Will you get cut? Probably. But don't let that discourage you. Bandage it up and keep going. You keep working with blades and guns and eventually you will not have any fear of them but you will develop a real respect for them. And the only way to get into this state is to train with live weapons.

So what techniques can you practice when using live weapons? Let's start with blades. You can substitute anything in for a blade as far as techniques goes because they're mostly all the same. Blade, bat, machete, stick, 2x4, bottle of beer, axe, pool stick and anything else you can swing strike, stab, hit and on and on. Get the picture?

If you know anything about Arnis, awesome, because all those techniques are great for practicing with blades. If you don't know Arnis, then no problem. Arnis makes use of sticks and blades for fighting and defending yourself. It also uses empty hand techniques but that's not the point right now. So if you're already familiar with Arnis, then when you go to train by yourself start switching your stick/blade choices around. Then go do your forms with the live blade in one hand. Actually striking something with whatever you're using is imperative at this point because you have to know how it's actually going to feel.

Don't start whacking the crap out of a tree cause your wife might get upset at you for hacking up her favorite tree. Instead go out and get an eight foot 4x4 at your local lumber store. Wrap some old cloths around it a few times. This way you can practice your slashes to see how deep you can slice into the clothing and also, how sharp your blades are. Never, never, never, let your blades get dull. If you have a dull blade then you don't respect the blade. And it's just plain embarrassing to have a dull blade anyway. So bury the 4x4 about two feet in the ground and then use that as your training dummy. If you really want to work on getting more out of the 4x4 then buy a 2x4 too and then cut two pieces off it that are about as long as your arm. You're going to have to make some angle cuts to attach them to the 4x4 so if you don't know how to do that then get someone to help. Place them on the 4x4 as if they were arms coming out from the body in a V like position. You don't have to put them at exactly the same level. You can put one high and one low just like someone would do if they're holding a knife in front of you. One idea I was fooling around with was making multiple holes up and down the 4x4. Then I would use bolts to attach the 2x4's into the 4x4. That way I could change the level of each arm as I needed to. Be creative and make something that works for you. The sky's the limit with this one.

When you start training with it make sure you hit it with as many angles as you can. Include forward swinging strikes, backhand swinging strikes, stabs, and don't forget about the butt end of your blade. The butt would be the end of the handle as in a smashing type strike. Imagine the 4x4 dummy being a person and attack the upper areas like the head and shoulders, the mid section like the side and chest areas, the arms if you put them on, and the lower section like the legs and groin areas.

Go slow at first and then build up speed. Don't hit it so hard that you imbed your blade in the 4x4 with every swing because that won't help you with the whole speed thing. At the very end you can do a heavy strike to finish the 4x4 off.

The whole point of training with live weapons is to get you used to them and making them a part of you. Once you have that then that is one less thing you have to worry about if actually confronted by a person with a real weapon. Will it take away all of the "holy shit" reaction if someone pops one out? No, but it will most certainly take away some of it and the faster you can regain your composure the better off you will be.

Let's move on to guns. One of the best training tools you can use to train with guns is the blank gun. As I said, they look like and function just like the real thing. So what can you do to practice with them? Hold them and dry fire, dry fire, dry fire. Dry fire is doing everything you would do when actually firing the gun except that it is unloaded. We would do this for weeks in Marine Corps boot camp. We also did this after boot camp as well. We would take them apart and put them back together all the time. We would carry them around everywhere. And we would dry fire. And after that we would move on to live fire training whether it was room clearing, urban warfare, jungle training, or whatever. We had our main and secondary and sometimes third weapons but they were usually the same weapons every time unless there was something special about whatever deployment we had to go on.

The main hurtle of a fear of guns is to actually hold them and use them. No other way around that one. It's funny that more people are afraid of guns than they are of knives. The knife can hurt someone in so many different ways but a gun is only dangerous right in front of that little hole. The barrel. That's it.

Don't believe me? Look at it this way. Give a kid a practice blade of any size and tell him to try to cut you in any way he wants to. You can try to move in and take it but if you tell him not to let you take it and try to cut you as many times as he can I guarantee that he will cut you several times with all kinds of weird movements before you can actually take his blade away.

Now I know you can't give a kid a real gun and say try to shoot me but maybe if you had a paint ball gun around then try that. I bet it will be harder for him to shoot you before you take the gun away. It's because the gun is only dangerous right in front of it. And most people need a ton of practice to get good at shooting. Not like a knife where you can just pick it up for the first time and do a ton of damage.

So whatever weapon you choose to carry, have respect for it but be in control of it. Clean it, make sure it is always in working order, and take care of it just as you would yourself. After all, it's an extension of you and if it's not yet then you need more training with it so it becomes part of you. You must be in charge of the weapon and not the weapon in charge of you. You are the one telling it where to go and how to move just as you would your hands, arms, and legs. You are its master.

The Marine Corps Rifleman's Creed says it all. It's about rifles but all of your weapons should be treated in the exact same way. Start saying this creed about all your weapons and you will start to understand how it's gotta be.

GET FOCUSED QUICKLY

The Rifleman's Creed

This is my rifle. There are many like it, but this one is mine. My rifle is my best friend. It is my life. I must master it as I must master my life.

Without me, my rifle is useless. Without my rifle, I am useless. I must fire my rifle true. I must shoot straighter than my enemy who is trying to kill me. I must shoot him before he shoots me. I will ...

My rifle and I know that what counts in war is not the rounds we fire, the noise of our burst, nor the smoke we make. We know that it is the hits that count. We will hit ...

My rifle is human, even as I, because it is my life. Thus, I will learn it as a brother. I will learn its weaknesses, its strength, its parts, its accessories, its sights and its barrel. I will keep my rifle clean and ready, even as I am clean and ready. We will become part of each other. We will ...

Before God, I swear this creed. My rifle and I are the defenders of my country. We are the masters of our enemy. We are the saviors of my life.

So be it, until victory is America's and there is no enemy, but peace!

MARINE CORPS!!!

5 MIND LIKE WATER BUT BRING THE FIRE

We've all heard the saying mind like water and it's a good one. It's about being calm inside because when you're calm the techniques that you know can come out and be used. The more un-calm we are the less we can access because we start to lose the fine motor skills necessary to pull off those kinds of techniques. Most of the fancier techniques require fine motor skills. Fine motor skills refer to the coordination between small muscles, like those of the hands and fingers, with the eyes. For example, when you are super angry and want to scream and there is a ton of adrenaline pumping you will notice that it's hard to coordinate your hands and fingers properly. That's why we start getting clumsy when we are that pissed off.

What's available if you're not calm during an altercation? Your gross motor techniques. Gross motor skills use the large muscles of the arms, legs, and torso so things like punching and kicking are possible. That's about all that you're going to be able to pull off. And if you go to the ground with someone in this state you won't be able to pull off any of those fancy more technical BJJ techniques. Your mind just won't have them available. Not unless you're calm anyway.

So that goes back to the saying "mind like water" or be like water or whatever like water. It encompasses being calm in the face of danger and being able to take on the form of whatever defense you need for any situation. Everything flows smoothly like water. And so on and so on.

Ok so that's all well and good until you get thrown a curve ball in the middle of an altercation. Remember what I said about real fights? Something about ugly? Yeah, they're ugly and quick and there are a ton of things that can go wrong.

Picture this. You're taking care of business with some dude that just tried to jack your girlfriend's purse or whatever scenario you want to come up with. You're handling him fine and using all sorts of fancy techniques because this guy doesn't seem to know that much about fighting. Maybe you're throwing him around and taking way too long to end the situation. Your mind and body are flowing just like water and you're in the zone. Every technique you call upon comes flowing out. You're ok, right? You have perfect calmness and can basically toss him around at will. Timing is on, techniques are on, and this is great right? At this point you're thinking you should become a superhero and fight crime and bad guy's right?

Then out of nowhere you get cracked in the back of your skull with an empty beer bottle. That was the guy's accomplice that was drinking a beer and just caught up with his buddy. Let's say you got lucky and didn't get knocked out right away but you can now feel the blood pouring out of your skull and running down your back and arms. You can feel it in your fingers and everything feels slippery and wet. Forget about trying those fancy fine motor skill techniques now with blood all over your hands and you still saying to yourself, what the hell just happened? The pain is intense and you look behind you and this guy that just cracked you is yelling that he's gonna mess you up bad for throwing his buddy around for so long. The other guy that you took so long to play around with is now getting his senses back and starts to yell at you as well and posture up.

Damn, this wasn't supposed to happen. I had mind like water and in the movies you always see this little Asian man just standing there all calm and then he kicks the crap out of everyone and goes back to standing there in all his glory and calmness.

Too bad you aren't in any movie right now. What should you do now? Well, first thing was that you should have taken care of the first guy immediately and gotten the hell out of there. Yeah, mind like water is a must but when you defend yourself you need to bring the fire. And bring it hard. Any type of violence brought upon you or your loved ones needs to be met with the same or greater level of violence as your attacker and it must be immediate. No screwing around. You need to have intent when you go after someone when defending yourself and hit them hard.

You will learn all kinds of things at a good dojo but real intent must be taken on by you. Hopefully you have heard about this at your dojo but even if you have listened to all your sensei's about it you will have to have the mindset to actually practice it and learn it. Sorry but no one at the dojo or any other place can change your mindset for you. This is something that YOU and you alone must accomplish.

I hear time and time again from people who don't train in the martial arts (and some who have) that martial arts don't work in a street fight. What's my opinion? They will absolutely work if you use the right techniques and have the right mindset and attitude. I know of many black belts who think that just because they earned their black belt that they can take on anyone. And then they get their asses handed to them and say that martial arts don't work and they usually end up quitting. I have also seen many fights where the guy who trains will fight like he is still at the dojo. There is no intent displayed in any of the stuff that he is trying to pull off. It usually looks like he is in the first round of a boxing match where the two opponents are trying to feel each other out but not land anything with any intent. Then he gets overpowered and ends up on the ground thinking to himself, what the hell just happened? What happened? Should have gone after him with intent. End it quickly and end it ugly. You're in the world of UglyDo now.

Great, so what does it mean to actually hit someone with intent? And if I hit someone with intent where do I hit him? There are many questions you can ask about defending yourself and how far should you take it. Let's face it, not all altercations require deadly force. Most of them don't. Unless you're doing law enforcement raids or an operator in the CIA or something, most of the time, you won't need to go that far. That said, how far you take it is based on the situation and your ability to recognize the level of force needed.

The local drunk at the bar might get loud and out of hand but you don't want to use deadly force but you definitely want to stop the situation based on what he does to you. Some of the techniques I have seen for dealing with the chest pumping, hand pushing, idiot requires you to wait for him to push you several times before you actually react. Why wait? The first time he pushes you, especially if you have properly recognized the situation and have your hands up in a "hey, I don't want to fight you" stance, he has already committed an assault and you have the right to defend yourself.

I say do not wait for that sucker punch to come out of nowhere. Your response should be immediate and violent. Immediate in the sense of right after he shoves you for the first time and violent in the sense of you need to match and overtake his level of violence. To not heed this advice is asking to get hurt badly.

You don't want to go punch for punch with anyone. Why take that chance?

You have no idea of his intentions and if he knocks you down you have no idea what he will do. Maybe start kicking you in the head leaving you paralyzed for life? Maybe actually kicking or hitting you so hard to end your life? Maybe leaving you for a trip to the hospital where you will need some sort of medical treatment? At the very best, leaving you with bruises all over your face and now you have to explain to your boss at work why you got into a situation like that in the first place.

So what did I mean about intent? In the dojo we all started out not wanting to really hit someone. We just wanted to practice punching kicking or whatever we just learned. That's fine because everyone has to start somewhere. Well what about when we have a few years under our belt and really want to start getting into realistic situations? Well, we have all heard the saying about practicing the way you would do it for real right? If no one has told you that then they should have and I'm telling you right now. Practice likes it real. PERIOD. And not just the techniques either. I'm saying practice the technique like it real, practice your mind like its real, and practice your attitude like its real. Practicing these three things will forge your intent. You will have your fire.

Let's start with the technique. I'm not saying you have to full on crank someone's arm out of their socket. But you should practice it as real as you can and right before you would snap their arm off then slow it way down and do the rest of it carefully. Or let your partner go and finish the technique full speed. Especially if your partner can't take a throw or fall and doing so would probably get him injured. This way you can actually go full bore and not injure anyone you're practicing with. Always finish a technique. If you continually practice a technique halfway then when you actually have to use it you will only be able to use up to the point where you stopped. The more times you practice this way will engrain it into your muscle memory and brain and you will have no problem when the time comes to pull the trigger for real.

I see way too many martial artists practicing like they're fooling around playing tag or hot potato. And when I see a black belt doing this I really want to walk up to them and punch them in the throat and scream, practice like its real! Maybe that will awaken them. Or get me kicked out of the dojo. Probably both but at least they're awakened now right? Whether they like it or not, all the lower belts are watching them and look up to them. They will copy whatever they do. So keep that in mind black belts.

So then we move on to mind. What do I mean by that? Your mindset has to be focused on the situation. Even in the dojo. Make it real. Don't look at your buddy as someone you always practice with but look at him as someone who wants to hurt or kill you. Whatever situation you're practicing for make your mind see it as that situation. Maybe you're practicing defending against someone taking a haymaker swing at you. Put yourself into a situation like a bar and some drunk guy mouthing off to everyone and running over to you and taking a big huge haymaker swing at you. Hear the loud music and all the talking and loudness. See the darkened bar area or lights flickering on and off like some dance club. Where ever you can picture yourself, USE IT. Maybe see a bunch of patrons or bar stools all over the place. You can then practice taking down your opponent in a confined area right? Keep him IN THAT SPACE when you drop him. Be there in that space in your mind. Even better, put some actual obstacles in the way or prop up some mats to make a small enclosed area to practice in.

You're probably never going to get into a real fight in a big open flat area with mats all over the place and perfect lighting and no sound right? Well, unless you're a real big jerk and want to take someone on for real at the dojo. Not recommended though. More likely, a confrontation will be in a place with space restrictions, stuff all over the place, and maybe you're kids or wife along with you. In the dojo you could however, turn the lights off, put in a couple weird lights or strobes, play some loud music, and throw a bunch of crap all over the place. Make it real and train like its real.

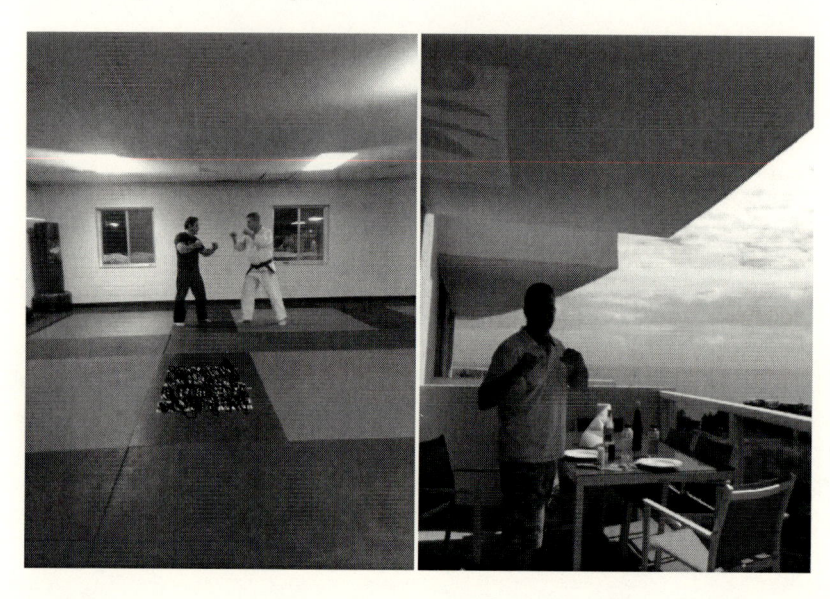

Lastly, practice your attitude. I know what you're probably thinking. That you have to be a big egotistical asshole right? No. Far from it. What I mean is almost the same as using your mind. Have the attitude like its real. There should be a noticeable change of look on your face. Why? Someone is ATTACKING you. You need to get serious and focused quickly. You think in a real situation your face is going to look like you're eating a burger? Hell no. You're going to either look scared shitless or you are going to look like you are ready and really focused on the situation and really pissed off that you're being attacked. I've been told on numerous occasions at the dojo that when they are supposed to attack me they say, why would I want to attack him, he looks like he is going to kill me. THAT'S the attitude I am talking about. And when I take them down I finish it. I'll usually punch them in the neck somewhere but see myself actually punching straight through their neck and using my kiai at the same time. And not some wimpy kiai. Mine are usually from the gut and more violent sounding. My daughter has told me that I need to calm down after doing a bunch of them. Train like its real.

And yes, you need the mind like water but on the outside you need the fire. Make whoever is attacking you pause and think twice before they come after you. Or if they have already attacked you then face them and make them think that they have just made a really big mistake.

I don't know how many times I was working on Buffalo's west side and I had some beer drinking crack head sitting on his porch taunting me and saying he was gonna kick my ass. I was calm and mind like water (most of the time anyway) but when I saw that they were actually walking toward me with some kind of drunken intent I immediately flipped that proverbial switch and became a fiery demon from hell and hit them with fiery intent.

The majority of the time when they saw the change, they would instantly stop and I could see it in their face they were thinking that they made a big mistake. The ones that didn't realize this definitely realized it after I was done with them.

So at the dojo make sure to practice everything. Fighting isn't just about throwing as many punches as you can. There is much more to it. Practice like its real.

And when you're being the attacker at the dojo, do your partner the favor of making it real for them. I hate seeing someone throwing a half ass punch that doesn't even come near their partner. When someone does this to me I just stand there, not moving, and ask them if they're attacking me or trying to catch a fly? Sometimes when I know my partner is not sure about hitting me (because way too my martial artists don't like to actually be hit), I tell them to hit me harder and harder until I think they have the right mindset. This also gets you used to being hit as well.

Speaking of being hit, let someone beat away on you. Take some punches once in awhile. Forge the fire. Let that white belt haul away on you because they're really good at the unexpected attacks and sometimes crazy attacks in the circle. The more you take the more you will be used to taking.

I love the more aggressive techniques. You tend to go straight in and get in the attackers space. You also take more hits this way but if you practice being hit and make sure you mitigate the hits so you don't take one square on then you should be fine.

Best way to learn how to get hit is to get a partner, put on some boxing gloves, and start slugging away. Super workout as well. This is a perfect way to build up your intent and not get too hurt. This will forge both the water and fire in you. The water because you need to stay calm always and fire because you need that intent when you're going to strike. You will also learn really fast how to cover up and mitigate those punches. Start bobbing and weaving to avoid the hits. I love to watch Mike Tyson and how he moves in the ring. His opponents have a very difficult time trying to hit this guy. He took the bob and weave to a whole new level.

Start with the bigger gloves, like 14oz or more, and then work your way down to the lighter ones. Each time you do this the punches will hurt more and more. This is a good thing. You have to feel them because in a real fight there are no gloves. Let your partner beat the crap out of you without you hitting him back. Just try to evade his strikes as much as you can. Try to work yourself into getting him into a clinch. Then release him and start again.

Why the clinch? Because in a real fight if someone is whaling away on you then you will need to do something to get in close to stop him from hitting you. Remember I said at one point that I don't like to trade hits back and forth? If you start trading punches with someone you have about a fifty percent chance of defeating your opponent if you use this strategy. I don't like those odds when in a street fight. If you know for sure you can knock him out with a kick or hit then go for it. But I would rather go in for the clinch and then work from there.

What can you do from the clinch? Well that's for another chapter but the whole point about fire is that it's intense. Bring the violence when needed because you're going to need it if you get attacked. Do you really think you're going to be able to talk your way out of someone attacking you if he's a meth head and needs money quickly? Not gonna happen. He does not care about you or your family or any reason why you might say he shouldn't take your money and maybe stab you in the process. He DOESN'T CARE ABOUT YOU.

It makes me laugh every time I hear someone talk about terrorists, especially the ones in the Middle East. Some will say that we just need to talk with them and be nice to them and they will leave us alone. Let's tell them at we are sorry and that America is bad and they're good. Let's give them whatever they want and they will leave us alone for good. Give me a break. The people who say this kind of nonsense obviously have never dealt with these kinds of people. These terrorists DO NOT CARE about you or your family or your money or your life. They want you dead because you do not worship their God. If you are not a part of their religion you must die. Period. No talking or negotiating is going to change their mind. Other than their ideology, they're no different than the meth head on the street that has run out of money to buy more meth. Both will kill you without a single thought about it.

My point is that no matter who is attacking, you will need to stay relatively calm so you can focus on what is going on around you and you will need to have the fire to ramp up the violence you are going to bring down on them for attacking you in the first place. You MUST be more violent than they are. Why do you think the saying, fight fire with fire, has been around for so long? Have some intensity in your life. Have you ever been to someone who was very old funeral? Have you ever heard someone say that whoever died still had the fire in his eyes? Be that person who still had the fire till the day he died

Now you know that the old adage of Mind Like Water is a must but what most of us forget about is the fire. Have the fire ready at all times. Don't be scared to up the violence on someone that is being violent with you. When you are doing your daily exercises, have a clear mind and focus but don't forget about the fire. Get an attitude and scream at the top of your lungs when you think you can't do anymore of what you're doing. And then do more.

Forge your water and fire because only you have the ability to teach yourself this.

6 TAKING DOWN GOLIATH

I've been asked on several occasions, how to take down the big guy. You know the guy. He's the guy that comes into the dojo and looks like he could fight with the World Wrestling heavyweights. Muscles on muscles and if he has a ton of tats then he looks even scarier. Probably add in a goatee or beard to top everything off. Just the guy you want to throw down with for the next hour you spend on the mats let alone out on the street. When they say partner up everyone around him picks someone else right away. But you didn't because you were looking down at your feet and not paying attention when they said partner up. Damn, now what? How am I going to survive this class?

You don't see too many videos or other information out there on this subject. There is some but a lot of it doesn't point out that you're fighting a wild beast that wants to eat you for a snack before going out to down a couple whole chickens and then get a few more bottles of roids from his dealer.

A lot of people, me included, get psyched out when facing a big guy. I had this problem for years in the dojo. Especially when I had to roll with big guys doing Judo or BJJ. Man, I would see that big guy and say to myself, how in the hell am I going to throw this guy over my shoulder? Well, that was the first problem. My mind was saying NO WAY.

We all know that boxers will try to intimidate their opponents before the fight even starts. One of my favorite boxers, Mike Tyson, used to say that he wouldn't take his eyes off his opponent when he was waiting to start the fight. He would literally stare at the other guy until the fight started. He said that once he saw his opponent look down, he knew that he was going to win the fight because he just successfully intimidated his opponent.

So the mind is the very first thing that will lose you a fight against a big dude. It's the same thing that will lose you a fight with anyone. Remember the mind like water but bring the fire? You need that here more than ever with the big guys. Whether it be a ground and pound, a standing slug fest, or a weapon attack. If your mind isn't in it and has given up before it even starts, then you're done. And in the case of a knife attack, you might as well just lie on the ground and let your attacker stab you a few dozen times till you bleed out.

On several occasions that I have had an altercation with a much bigger dude and he was getting in my face and yelling and I knew that he was going to start a fight, I would have to match his violence and go above and beyond it. Deescalating the situation is a much better idea but if you know that he is going to start swinging at some point then you have to do something. And that something is to make him second guess his decision to kick your ass.

So far his violence level was just yelling a bunch of nonsense and him trying to build up the anger to actually initiate the fight. These guys usually want people to see them so they can show off how big and intimidating they are. They also like to get you set up for sucker attacks. You know, like looking around or looking back and then the big haymaker comes from nowhere? You need to have your mind at rest during this kind of thing but sometimes, if it can't be deescalated, you need to do something.

Now when I say match his violence, you can take that in two different forms. The first would be to go into psycho mode and match his anger with your own and go beyond his. This is risky but it has worked for me on several occasions. Was I scared? Hell yeah. And after he backed down I said to myself holy crap, thank God he backed down. Now this won't always be the case. If he has a bunch of his people around he might say to himself that he can't back down because of some ego shit he has in his head. And now all of his peers are watching.

The other way to handle this is to remain perfectly calm but aware of everything. You cannot show any kind of fear whatsoever when doing this. Look in his eyes like you're looking into his soul. If you know anything about the thousand yard stare then that's what I am talking about. Don't say anything and don't make any facial expressions. Be very careful that he doesn't get too far into your space. Don't engage in the chest bumping crap either. That goes for the psycho mode too. Again, be prepared if he doesn't back down.

Hopefully though, in either case, he will back down. I have employed both methods and I have had success with them. That' doesn't mean they will always work. When they don't, you have to be prepared. You have to be confident in your abilities. Your mindset has to be rock solid. That's the first thing that needs to be worked on and built up.

So if the mind is the first thing to work on then what's the second thing? Well, you have to have some sort of technique and knowledge of self defense/martial arts to fight a guy like this. You don't want the big guy to get a hold of you. Especially in the beginning when he has all his stamina. I'm not saying don't ever let him grab you, I'm just saying don't let him wrap you up. If you're good at let's say, Judo, then grip fighting with a big guy might be practical. Just don't think you're going to muscle him around much. And if you're a good Judo player you already know this. There is a reason why Judo has weight classes.

Any technique you use MUST not be a lazy technique. What do I mean by a lazy technique? Well, remember fighting someone in the dojo that was clearly below your skill level? Maybe you got paired up with some mid level guy. It was no problem to go right through them right? Some can surprise you but most of the time not. Well if we keep on fighting these guys all the time and not challenging ourselves with more skilled practitioners or BIGGER DUDES, then our technique can easily get lazy and sloppy. Why? Because we will start to cut corners and not really do the technique like it's supposed to be done. When you fight someone who is just learning you can get away with that because even the most basic techniques you throw at them they won't see coming. They're new and just learning. If you fight a really big guy with lazy technique you will be defeated. They have the ability to muscle through a lot of techniques if they are lazy techniques being used on them.

So now you ask, ok, I have no way out and I got to fight this guy. What do I do? Well I can tell you right now that you don't want to go blow for blow with this guy. Bad, bad, idea. The range of a bigger guy will most likely be more than your range. So if you're both punching at the same time he will get to you before you get to him. You have to be very mindful of the distance. You want to keep him out of his striking range. Move, move, move and do not let him get a hold of you.

More than likely he will be coming after you swinging away with everything he's got to try to strike you. It will seem like a barrage of strikes but just keep on moving. Bob and weave and move. To slow him down you can use some kicks. Your leg has more range than his punches so use them. But you will only want to use high percentage kicks. No fancy stuff unless you are really good at them and even then I wouldn't risk it. Not at the beginning of the fight anyway.

So what kicks would I use? The front push kick and the modified roundhouse kick. And I know what you're saying about both of them. I have seen the reasons not to use them but the ones that I use are better for this kind of altercation. They're both from Muay Thai the way they are executed.

The front push kick or Teep is used all the time in Muay Thai. It's basically used to create distance for other follow-up kicks or strikes and to also keep your opponent at bay. If your opponent is coming at you with everything then you want to move a lot and also use the Teep. This will make him think twice about coming at you full bore. It is like a front snap kick but you will use more of a pushing motion and your upper body will lean back as you kick forward. Try to keep the kick around the pelvic or lower abdomen areas. Using it to check their leg as they're moving forward is also good but it's a smaller target and can slip off and put you in a bad position. And remember to kick with intent. Like you're kicking in a door. What will all this do? It will absolutely slow him down which is what you want. Give you some breathing room.

If you want to sprinkle in some Muay Thai roundhouse kicks to the outside of the upper leg then do it but do it right. Don't overextend and hit him with the top of your foot as this can damage your foot. Hit him with your shin if possible but no lower than your upper ankle. Try to drive the kick in a downward fashion into the outside of his thigh. Muay Thai roundhouse kicks are much different than regular roundhouse kicks. It's more of a whipping action than a snapping motion. You have to spin on the ball of your feet and it can almost rotate 180 degrees if you do it right. Stay balanced and upright and throw your arm on the kicking side down as you will get more torque. The torque, if you're doing it correctly, will start at your pivoting foot and then move all the way up to your mid section and on through your whole body with your kicking leg whipping into his leg. If you do the arm throw then keep your shoulders up to protect your chin. After you make contact then return your leg as fast as you can so your opponent can't grab on to it.

So you've gotten this far without getting knocked out. Now what? Well at this point it shouldn't have taken so long. Remember this is not a fight in the ring, it's a fight on the street. Big guys tend to wear down quickly and expend a lot of energy up front. Not always the case but usually is. Wearing a big guy down can be like 45 seconds to a minute. How do you know he is wearing down? Watch his hands as they will start to drop. Listen to his breathing and look at his facial expressions. There will be a noticeable change of look in his face. It will go from pure rage to damn, I'm tired.
Look for the over extension that will start to happen because he doesn't want to get kicked anymore. Wear him down.

Once you know he is winded, it's now the time to take a more offensive approach. You will need to move in very quickly and grab on. What I mean is to get some sort of clinch going. A clinch is a two handed grip where you wrap your two hands around the back of his head/neck area. You can then start to pull his head down and in toward your chest. He can still strike you but you won't take the whole force of the punch.

What? You didn't think you were going to get hit at all? Put that nonsense out of your mind right now. You WILL get hit in an altercation. It's how you mitigate those hits that matters. And again, I already discussed taking hits at the dojo so you should be used to taking some kind of punishment right?

Once you have him in the clinch its time to punish him. At close range like the clinch the best weapons to use are the elbows and knees. Quickly smashing multiple elbows into his neck and chin area are a must. And since you're still maintaining the clinch, we can now drop his head further down and start multiple knee strikes to the face. Repeat as necessary.

If the altercation is still not over after that then you will need to take him down. Whatever technique you use, you must end up on top. Big guys are great candidates for foot sweeps. Especially if they're already winded. It's a great way to take someone down and still be standing right above them ready to bash their skull in (not that I am saying to do that).

If he is on the ground and you're over him then you can, if you're a proficient grappler, go down with him and submit him. If you're not a good grappler then I would start striking some vulnerable areas like the neck, armpit, genitals, knees or other joints, or anywhere you know there is not a lot of muscle protecting those spots. You need to end it at this point and not let it drag on.

Another great way to bring a big guy down is to go after the knees. Yes, this is considered dirty. If you care about that then you probably shouldn't be reading a book like this. Going after knees will stop just about anyone. But it can stop a big guy in his tracks because the bigger they are the more weight and stress they put on their knees. The bigger they are the harder they fall is true. The knees are the reason for it. The drill in the first part of this book talked about knees and how to go after them. Make that knee go in a direction that it wasn't intended to go. There is also nothing that says you have to wait until they hit you to hit them back. Yes, I know that means that if you initiate the first strike then in the eyes of the law you're now the aggressor but if you know he is going to come at you and think you can take him down right away then do it.

If you really want to take someone down quickly then kick them in the balls. Yup, another dirty tactic but hey, this is a street fight/altercation right? The only thing about using this tactic is that if you miss it will greatly piss him off and he might then use techniques that he wasn't planning on using in the first place. So if you're going to go after him first then make it count. Then get the hell out of there.

I know the chapter was about fighting a big guy but all the techniques I will talk about in this book will work against little or big guys. If it doesn't work against anyone I really have no use for it. Altercations are crazy enough without having to think which techniques to use depending on if they're big or little or fat or muscular or on crack or whatever. I just want a technique that works with everyone. Most good techniques are also ugly techniques. That's fine with me. Don't discard techniques because they aren't cool enough for you. Trust in UglyDo my friend.

So after all this are you asking if there is a better way? Sure, don't fight him and get the hell out of there. Or say you're sorry and ask him if you can buy him a beer. I've done this. Especially if I was the asshole and started it in the first place. Do whatever it takes to deescalate the situation. That goes with any kind of altercation. But again, if you can't get out or you have family around then do something. But whatever you do, do it with intent. Bring the fire and get it over and done with as quickly as possible. And with the big guys don't come at them with lazy technique. Matter of fact, don't ever use lazy technique whether you're training or actually fighting. Practice everything like its real.

7 FIGHT LIKE A GIRL

One of the things I wanted to write about but didn't have a clue or knowledge of was that of a woman's perspective on self defense and situations that are usually exclusive to women. Trying to get into the head of a woman on these subjects can be tough and we as guys usually can't understand fully the scope of their fear, thoughts, and emotions (don't even try to understand a woman's emotions). So I thought to myself, who I could recruit to help me write a chapter on this, and it was right in front of my eyes. My daughter Rebecca. She has been in the dojo with me since she was born. First starting out just running around the dojo with her little brother Zach and then stepping onto the mats for the first time to study Judo. Then a little later she picked up Isshinryu karate and earned her black belt at 18 years old. I can tell you as a father, seeing my daughter get her black belt was one of the proudest days of my life.

So, as her father who had been teaching her all the self defense I could, I knew that she had a solid knowledge of the multiple facets of protecting herself. I believe that the best thing a father can give to his daughter is the ability to defend herself and to at least give her the tools to be able to handle any situation whether that be self defense or anything else.

Looking back I do hope I focused on some of the other aspects of life and didn't give her the, don't trust anyone, attitude that I have. It's good to enjoy life without always having to look over your shoulder.

So I asked Rebecca to write a few things that would be from the perspective of a woman. So without further adieu, here are her thoughts:

> First off, I'd like to share an incident that happened to me awhile

back.

The summer of 2018 was coming to a close and one of the traditions of a nearby beach is having a massive bonfire, otherwise known as the Boat Burning. It's held right before Labor Day as a sign to everyone that the summer is essentially over. What happens is they build a boat out of wood, have a few hundred people sign it with a Sharpie, and then burn it to the ground. People start gathering at about 10pm long after it gets dark and there is a bar right at the entrance of the beach this is held. As I'm sure you can imagine people like to use this opportunity to get way too intoxicated. This is a foreshadowing and maybe should have been a sign for me at the time to think about my surroundings a bit more thoroughly, but I did not, and that is why I get to tell you this today.

I attended this event with my father and a few others. Several hours went by as a few hundred people gathered around the burning boat. The crowd started to dwindle as the night went on. It was about 1am when my dad told me he was getting tired and that we should probably head back. I said I didn't want to leave quite yet and even after about three hours of just standing around the fire, it was still entertaining to me. I had also just turned 18 a few weeks prior and thought I'd be ok. He considered this and told me I was probably old enough to stay by myself for a little while longer. I wouldn't be completely alone at the fire but by then, most of the crowd had left. Most people either went home or to the bar which was about fifty yards away. There were also security people there who were really just lifeguards in shirts that said SECURITY on them. So much for security I guess.

Shortly after my Dad left I started to chat with some of the security people. They were actually interesting, cool, and I liked talking with them, aside from the fact that they didn't really do their given jobs.

A few more minutes went by and I was still talking to security. We were chatting random nonsense and typical small talk. All of a sudden some dude comes walking down from the bar and inserts himself into our conversation. Now, I consider myself to be somewhat extroverted and don't mind talking to different people or making friends, however, this dude wasn't exactly giving me the best feeling. He was also standing about a foot away from me while the rest of us were spaced out comfortably. He kept talking and was obviously very drunk not to mention he had an empty beer in his hand. I inched away from him a bit as one does when they're uncomfortable, and he moved closer with me. Of course, me being a non confrontational shy 18 year old girl, I waited for one of the other guys to hopefully pick up on this and say something. They did not.

Finally, the conversation with this random guy sounded like it was about to come to an end and he says some drunk farewell to the security guys and then to me. He then turned around and right as he was about to walk away, smack! This drunken asshole really had the audacity to spank me. Not cool.

Now, as someone who has been doing martial arts since I was little, one might think I tried to beat this guy into oblivion, black-belt-girl style. Maybe I teach him a needed lesson or made it clear that he messed with the wrong person right? No. Not even close.

I completely froze and stood there like an idiot letting him walk away. I thought to myself, did I really just get sexually assaulted? I looked at the security guys, who just watched this entire thing unravel and waited for them to do something as they should have, but they did nothing. A few seconds went by as the guy started to walk up the beach towards the bar. At this point I was debating if I should go and attack him but shy and just-barely-legal me didn't want to make a scene. I was also afraid of getting in trouble for attacking someone but looking back at the context it seemed kind of silly. One of the security guys then said "do you want us to get him?" I ignored him and decided that I wanted to do something about it myself.

At this point, he had walked almost all the way back up to the entrance of the beach which was about 150 feet away. I started running up the sand which was quite difficult as you can imagine and finally, I got a few feet behind him and tapped him on the shoulder, still unsure of what I wanted to do to him at that point. He turned around and I slapped him in the face as hard as I could. He was still very drunk and couldn't hold his balance so he immediately fell to the ground. The few people that were walking by turned around to look at me wondering what the hell just happened. They probably just assumed he deserved it as they said nothing and kept walking.

I went back down to the now almost dead fire like nothing had occurred and one of the security guys asked if I was okay. I said I was fine but in my head I was so upset that they didn't do anything about it. Someone, who was actually a security guard, then came down and also asked if I was okay and informed me that the guy had been removed.

Shortly after this incident my Dad came back to the fire. It had only been about fifteen minutes since he left but he said he got a bad feeling and wanted to check in. I told him what happened and he was pretty enraged, as one might be, and asked if the guy was still around and to point him out. Lucky for that guy that he was escorted out by police and did not have to take a beating by my now pissed off Dad.

This was one of those "out of nowhere" incidents that my Dad always warned me about and said that sometimes things happen and you just have to be prepared for them.

Looking back on the whole incident I do think I was prepared. It may not seem like it since I didn't do much in reaction and even froze, but I really do think that I was prepared. I had more than enough skill and training to protect myself in that moment but I didn't have a game plan, not to mention the confidence to carry it through. It was one of those things that you knew could happen at any moment but still shocks you when it does. I still kick myself over it but at the end of the day, not many people are thinking about and preparing for an attack at any given moment. It's just not realistic. So, while I wish I did more, I understand that it was a relatively normal reaction.

In a way, I'm almost thankful for that experience. Even as someone who has practiced martial arts for many years, it's still hard to think that something can happen to you at any moment. However, I am certain that if something like this happens again, the guy won't be as lucky.

If there's one thing over a decade of training in martial arts has given me its confidence. It has given me confidence in my day to day life, how I carry myself, my strength, and my worth. It may not have seemed like I did very much in the retaliation at the beach, but I did do something. I decided in that moment what I wanted to do and I went after it.

I'm obviously not saying you can't have confidence naturally or through other means, because you absolutely can. However, I'd be lying if I said martial arts didn't help a great deal. Martial arts are a huge part of my life and I'm glad it's that way. However, I will say it's not everything.

Can I go through a dark alley in a bad part of town in the middle of the night? No, I'm scared of the dark. Can I jump into a windowless white van without fear? No, small spaces make me uncomfortable. Could I hold my own if a group of five plus people were to attack me with weapons? Most likely not, but that would be very badass. I'm not invincible. Nobody is. Your set of skills can only take you so far but in a worst case scenario, I'd much rather go out fighting than cowering. Now, worst case scenarios aren't usually what happen, and to me, that makes it more worth it to at least try training at some point. For me, knowing that training and investing time now could save me down the line just motivates me to keep going.

I feel like my experience as a woman in martial arts isn't very much different than that of a man's. Or at least what I think it would be like, anyway. I wouldn't know. I am not a man. Aside from people maybe not expecting the average female to indulge in such a thing or sometimes classmates being afraid of snapping me in half if they work with me? It doesn't seem like it's that different. I love what martial arts have done for me in my life and I think that men and women alike should try it at least once in their life. Coming from someone who has done it for so long it might seem a bit biased, however, you could very well find some value in it. If not, at least your friends might think you're cool.

Rebecca

Rebecca makes a lot of good points. An altercation can happen anywhere and just because you have skills doesn't mean you're going to react the way you think you would react. There are actually three responses to a stressful dangerous situation. They are Fight, Flight OR Freeze. We've all heard of the first two but freezing and not being able to do anything can happen too. It can happen to anyone and many of us have felt it. And I don't care how tough you think you are it can happen to the best of us. Also, being aware can be a good thing in your life but don't let it take over your life. Just work on getting it a better but still being able to turn it off when applicable.

Incidences like the one that happened to my daughter are the kinds of things that you will normally run into. If you're being violently attacked on a daily basis then you're going into the wrong places. As a women going into a bar your chances of running into a jerk like the one Rebecca ran into are high.

Now, I think the title of this chapter might raise a few eyebrows but I believe that a lot of the stuff recommended for women to do if confronted by an attacker is the same kind of stuff that men can do as well. What, screaming and yelling is not cool enough for you? You want to stand up and fight like a man? Fine. But just be aware that it could be your last fight if you're not careful. There is always someone bigger and badder out there. And I'm not talking about fighting with one of your buddies because he got too drunk and said something stupid to your girlfriend. I'm talking about someone who really wants to hurt you.

So why don't they have a special men's self defense classes? They do. It's the regular training at a dojo or gym. Women have special self defense classes because like it or not, they have a greater chance of having someone attack them whether that be an attempted robbery, rape, or their boyfriend or husband beating or abusing them in some shape or form. Myself having a daughter this has always been on my mind and one of the reasons I made it a priority to take her with me to train at the dojo.

I would like to see anyone that trains alongside women to not treat them like they're breakable. What does that mean? It means that you need to go after them as an attacker would. Don't show off and make it a point to just crush them because you think it makes you look cool or impressive, because it doesn't. Come after them so they can feel what it's like to be attacked. Make them work to get out of it because if it happens for real then they need to fight and fight harder than a guy in the same situation would have to. Sorry, but it's true. Remember, they're going to do IT like they trained IT so make sure they train it right.

The best thing a women being attacked can do is to keep on moving and fighting. Scream and yell. Go completely nuts. Most attacks on women the attacker doesn't want the fight or exposure of someone seeing what he is doing. If it's someone you know attacking you then you need to do whatever it takes to get out of there. A lot of times, unfortunately, the guy attacking his girlfriend or wife doesn't really care if someone see's him. He will be full of rage and will just want to hurt or kill his victim. Sad but true again.

So what can a woman do to train properly that's different from a guy? First thing is to find a guy to train with that won't treat you like a flower. All the training in this book applies to women too. I just see a lot of guys hold back when they go up against a woman. I've been told several times by women in my dojo that they like to train with me because I don't hold back. That doesn't mean I purposely try to hurt anyone, it means I treat them like one of the guys and train hard. That doesn't mean you have a new female come in to the dojo and beat the crap out of her. You have to work them into it until they get used to everything and know a little bit about what they're doing and can handle.

A lot of women and some men as a matter of fact, will come in to train and are scared to hit someone. I let them hit or kick me as hard as they can until I can't take it anymore. Once I see that they're going full power then I tell them that's the one. That's how you need to hit or kick someone when you mean it. It's also training me to take hits and manage the pain.

Some of the feistiest women I've trained with are also the smallest women I've trained with. It doesn't matter the size, color, or gender when it comes to being a badass. You never know who knows what. What the feistiest women have that others don't is the sheer will to get out of a bad situation. They will keep on moving and hitting and doing whatever they need to do to get out.

I was helping with a women's self class a while back and I ran into two complexly different types of women. When I attacked the first one she instantly dropped to the ground and started crying. I was like, what happened? Are you alright? I hadn't even grabbed her at that point. I just got her up against a wall and started to yell at her. Apparently she had a bad encounter in which someone attempted to rape her. I don't know if it actually happened or not as I didn't really pressure her to tell me anything but she did let me know pretty much what happened. So in that case, we had to slow way down and work with her a lot more to get her to the point where she wasn't going to break down at the first sign of aggression.

The next one was in a similar situation and as soon as I started pushing her against the wall she went completely bonkers. She started screaming at the top of her lungs and hitting me with elbows, fists, knees, and then grabbed my head and twisted my head gear so far that the opening was in the back of my head. I was on the ground in a turtle position taking all sorts of shots. The instructors had to step in pretty quickly as I thought I just instantly became the victim. She apologized but I told her there was no need to apologize and how she reacted was perfect. It completely caught me off guard but that was the point. In a real situation like that you need to make your attacker feel like a victim. Turn it around on them. Your reaction to a violent event has to match their violence and that violence has to be immediate. If you don't want to be violent then don't get into a bad situation. Thing is, we don't get to pick when we get attacked.

So there are all types of women out there and when they come to you for help with training you need to take it seriously because their life might depend on it one day.

8 BASIC TECHNIQUES

Ok, so I wanted this chapter to include techniques that you can use in any situation and be fairly good at it in a short amount of time. You will still need a fair amount of training with them in order to become good at them but it shouldn't take long. It's one of those things that get better with practice. Your odds at coming out of an altercation without getting too beat up will increase the more you practice. Best place to train in my opinion is a legit dojo. How do you find a legit place to train? Well, go ask around. Take a few classes and see if you like the atmosphere and people. You will want to find someplace that does as much as possible. Standing, clinching, and grappling, and whatever else you want to add in. The more the better. I don't want to go on and on about how to find a good place to train because that's not to object of this book. Just find a good place that you like and get along with everyone.

So where do I start with the basic techniques? Let's start with protecting yourself right off the bat. If you're getting pummeled you don't want to get knocked out and then have to worry about how far this guy is going to take beating on you right? I don't know how many times over the years while training kids and adults alike, when they're getting manhandled by someone, they will go into a protective shell. What I mean is that they turn their back on an opponent and cover up their head. Anyone see a problem with this? Yeah, they just turned their back on someone who is beating the hell out of them. They can then haul off on you without them being worried about any retaliation at all because your back is turned. They can even grab you and throw you all over the place or even choke you out from behind. NEVER give your attacker your back. EVER.

Let's add on to the whole thing about turning your back on someone. You

BASIC TECHNIQUES

also don't want to keep on backing up either. That just gives the attacker more room and leverage to really come down on you. Always take the fight back to him. That means driving back into him taking away his space. Make HIM back up. If you're backing someone up they won't be able to strike you with their full force. It has to do with physics and with the amount of force you can produce while momentum is against you. When you're going into someone you will still need to protect your head. The best cover up I use is to take one of your hands and reach up and grab the back of your head keeping your palm on the middle to top of the ear. Keep your elbow up and tucked in. Make sure you can still see your attacker while tucking your head. Keep your knees slightly bent so you can utilize movement. Use the other arm in the same way for the other side. Point your elbow at your attackers face and then start driving into him. If you have both of your hands up then point the elbow that you're leading with towards him. A lot of the time he will end up hitting your elbow with a punch. Bad for him. This will hurt him a lot more than it's going to hurt you. Once you have blocked one or two of his punches then you should start moving in. And remember, keep moving. Bobbing and weaving is great for this tactic. Once you have gotten close enough to him drive your elbow into his face.

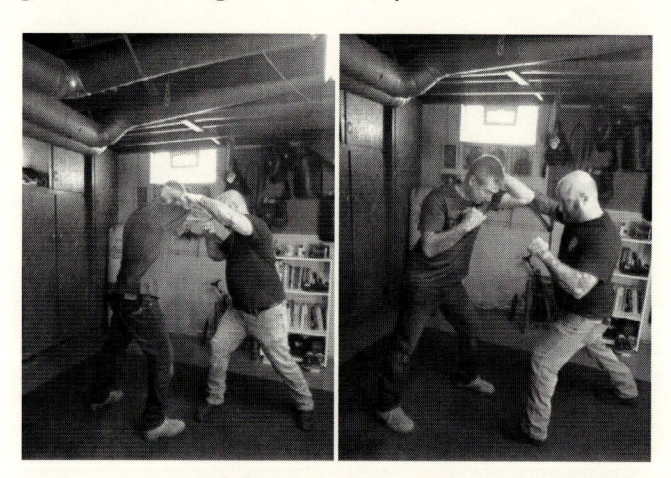

So you're probably saying, well, if I cover up my head, what about getting hit in the mid section? Well, guess what? You probably will get hit in the mid section. Remember what I said in chapter 5? You better have been letting those people take some hits on you.

A good way to practice this technique is to go to your dojo and ask someone to spare with you. Everyone loves to spar at the dojo. Trust me, if you go into any dojo on this planet and ask if anyone would like to spar for a bit, you will not have any problem getting someone to spar with you.

Don't forget to have an explanation after you tell them what you want to do. You'll see what I mean.

So once you have someone to spare with, tell them to put on some hand protection. I would recommend having them put on something that you would be able to handle if taking a real punch with. So once he has them on tell him to just come after you and just beat the crap out of you. I would start slow and then build up to full real speed. Yes, he is going to beat the crap out of you. Guess you can call it the Beat Down drill. But that's the point. Remember when I said have him put on hand protection that you could handle taking a real hit with? Well I meant it. Don't try to be cool and tell everyone that you can handle something you know you can't. Work up to it. I would start out at one minute rounds. Maybe two or three rounds to start out. Then build up to more time, rounds, and lighter hand protection. If you can't finish a round don't be too proud to tap out. Then just remember how long you lasted and then try to beat it the next time. This is an awesome exercise that will train you in so many things. It will train you how to take a hit, it will train you to always move and watch your partner, it will show you how to use you whole body and specifically the elbows as a weapon, it will teach you how to think quickly, it will show you how to protect yourself, and one of the more important things is that it will show you just how much guts you have deep down.

Just remember, don't take more of a beat down than you can handle. Just starting the Beat Down drill shows some serious guts. So be proud.

Now some of you might be saying, are you out of your mind? You want me to go to my dojo and just get beat down for the next what? Three weeks? YES, that's what I'm saying. Maybe then you would find out real quick that you need to start training like you mean it. You know who you are!

So now that I have probably pissed someone off, let's get into the next basic technique. If you liked the last one then you're really going to love this one. It's the good old bob and weave. This is another awesome drill and the training behind it will have a ton of good lessons for you.

So bobbing and weaving consists of you rapidly moving your upper body and head around to avoid a strike to it. This is all by a combination of moving from side to side and up and down, all while keeping your center and your balance as best as possible. Really, that's it. Anyone can do it but it takes some practice to really get good at it.

How can you train to do this? That's an easy one too. Go to your dojo. I know that you're thinking, what? Is this going to be Beat Down drill part two? No its not. I will call this one the Iron Mike drill in recognition of my favorite boxer, Mike Tyson.

Again, I would recommend having your opponent put on something that you would be able to handle if taking a real punch with. You thought that the idea for bobbing and weaving is to avoid taking hits? Yes, it is, but you will most certainly take some shots because you bobbed or weaved the wrong way. This is all about instinct and reading your attacker. You will get better as you go and practice more and more.

I would start at one to three, one minute rounds. Then build up to more time, rounds, and lighter hand protection as in the last drill. Have your partner put on whatever hand protection you chose, and just try to hit you. Your only task is to bob and weave and not let him hit your head. If you can see that you're bobbing and weaving the wrong way you can use any parry or side step that you need to not get hit in the face. If he tries to hit you anywhere else you're just to take the hit. This will not only get you thinking really quickly but you will also be taking more shots which will build your toughness. It will also teach you seeing your opponent's strikes and the coordination for your movements. Both the Beat Down and the Iron Mike drills are also good for the partner because they're going to get a hell of a workout as well. Move, move, move, and then just keep on moving. Our hand eye coordination takes a huge dip on moving targets. It's been studied in physics and other sciences so keep that head moving.

So what could possibly be next? One of my favorites, The Clinch drill. You will need to know the clinch if you have to fight someone and end it quickly. This drill will show you how to use the clinch in many different ways. You can use it from far away as a way to get in closer or to take someone down. You can use it if you're close up as in a smothering clinch or a way to get to a more dominant position. You can use it to set up more advanced techniques talked about in the next chapter. You can use it to bring up your opponents head down for elbow strikes, knee strikes, or whatever strikes you want to maneuver him into. You can even use it to completely wear him down without having to throw a punch. There are tons of good things to learn from it.

Let's first describe what the basic clinch is. That way you can adopt your clinch into anything else you want to use it for. Face your opponent and put both of your hands behind your opponent's neck. They should be over lapping and cupped with more of the pressure from the pinky side when trying to keep hold of him and more index finger side then trying to maneuver him. Both of your arms should be inside your opponent's arms. I start with hands behind the neck because it's easier to get there than it is to get to the next step right away. It's going to start making your opponent tired because he is going to immediately want to pull back. Once you get both hands back there start moving them up toward the back of your opponents head while also starting to open your fingers up while still having them cupped. Start pulling him down and clamping your elbows together to try to cut off circulation in the side of his neck. Now you can pull him around and maneuver him for all kinds of good stuff now.

So that's the basic clinch. How do you get there? Well there's where the Clinch drills come in.

Get a partner that you can work with. Start out facing each other and then each of you try to work your way into the dominant position (both arms

BASIC TECHNIQUES

inside your opponent's arms and hands around the back of his head). Then try to keep him there and maneuver him around to your liking. I like to start out by getting at least one hand on the back of his neck and then working from there. The other arm is usually going for a grip on his other arm and then working back up to get the dominant position. You really want to be close so you don't take any real shots from him. When you're ready to strike you can maneuver him away to create the distance you need to pull off whatever technique you're going to use. Once you get that under your belt then add in knee strikes and elbows. The main thing about the clinch is that it really wears down your opponent because all he wants to do it lift his head up and get out of the clinch so he doesn't eat any knees or elbows. The longer you keep him in the clinch and his head is getting pulled down the more energy he is going to use to try to get out.

Now that we have a good grasp at upper body stuff let's look at the lower body. Kicks come right to mind. What are the best basic kicks to use in a fight? Well, it's whatever kick you can actually pull off but I have three favorites that I have and would use in an altercation but one is a little more advanced so I'll keep it for that chapter. The first one is a modified front heel kick. The second one is right from Muay Thai, the front push kick (or teep). They're both great for keeping an aggressive attacker at bay but the modified front heel kick can absolutely end a fight if it's done right. These are really good for ass kicking so I'll call the drill the Kick Ass drill.

Let's look at the front heal kick. Face your partner and take your right leg and lift your knee, facing it to your right side, up as far as it can go and then slam it into, preferably, the outside knee or the upper front knee with the inside heal or arch of your foot. Lean back a little when you're doing this as it can add some serious power to it. This is a great way to take someone out when at close range. If you don't break his knee you will absolutely do some painful damage to it. And if he is coming at you full on and you hit him with this kick it can absolutely destroy his knee and probably all sorts of tendons.

The second way I like to use it is more of an aggressive distraction to set someone up for more advanced techniques. I call a technique advanced if you have to do something before hand to distract your attacker to actually pull off your technique. There are all kinds of techniques that are being taught out there that need some sort of distraction to actually work. That's why when you learn a really cool technique that you think is really awesome and you practice with a willing participant, it works all the time but when you actually use it against a resisting partner it doesn't work so well.

So my favorite distraction is if someone gets a hold of you or you get a hold of them you can take your foot, turn your toes to the outside, and then slam your inside heel as hard as you can into their shin. Doesn't matter which shin, just hit it as hard as you can. If you have a little time to spare you can do this and then rake your heel down their shin and then jamb into their foot. Most of the time you aren't going to have time to do this because you only have a couple of seconds to do whatever you're going to do next. You will absolutely feel them loosen up their grip so you can then proceed on to a more advanced technique.

BASIC TECHNIQUES

If you don't believe distractions work then ask someone to hold on to your arm or shoulder or whatever. Do not tell them what you're planning on doing as a distraction will not work if they know what you're going to do. That's the whole point right? Then, kick them in the shin. Don't have to kick them super hard as they might not like you after that. You can even do a sudden scream in their face instead. Whatever you do just notice the release of pressure of whatever they were holding on to. Might be a big release or it might be a small one. Either way it will be just enough to let you move or get out of that grip and do something. So if you kick someone with a heel to their shin you're most absolutely going to distract them. Don't forget, out in the street we are wearing shoes so a heel is going to hurt.

The next kick is the front push kick, or Teep as it's known in Muay Thai. I know what some practitioners are going to say about a push kick in a real fight. That it's dangerous to use in a fight because you can catch the leg or get pushed back or whatever. Ok well, yeah, in a dojo where you're lackadazilly (yes that's a word) coming at someone who is going to kick you, you can catch that kick all day. But an attacker is not going to come at you without some intent to hurt you. They're coming at you to take your head off. So when someone is driving into you and you oppose that force with a greater kicking force then you will be inflicting some damage on him. And sure, if you keep on doing that kick over and over and not doing anything else to end the fight then yeah, they will be ready for it. So don't mess around and take your attacker out as quickly as possible. Kind of what I've been saying throughout this whole book.

The front push kick can be executed by either lead leg or rear leg. You will want to bring your knee up in front of you as high as you can go while being on the ball of your other foot on the ground. The kick should be snapped out there like you're kicking in a door and your hips and foot on the ground should be extended a little to generate more power. Opposite side arm should be up protecting your face and the other arm should swing down to generate leverage and even more power. Once you kick your target you can quickly bring your foot back to where it started or drop it right to the ground so that you can start another technique. I like to drop it right in front of my opponent and then go in for an elbow or punch to the neck.

How would you practice the Kick Ass drill? There is a way to drill this and still be safe, relatively speaking. So for the attacker, he would start by taking deliberate steps toward you but always have his legs bent in toward you. This way, if you do tap him, he will be expecting it and have his legs bent to take the hit. You as the defender would go slow and go right into his knee, just resting on it. You can go as fast as you want but need to have some sort of control to stop it before you go through his knee. I would suggest some knee padding for this one as it doesn't take much to damage a knee. The same thing would go for the front push kick. Your partner will just start walking and running aggressively into you for you to slow him down with the push kick.

This drill is all about trust and working up the speed. It's the attacker that is going to be used like a human kicking bag. He is just going to be taking kick after kick. Work up the speed and do as much as your partner can take at a time. It will certainly build up his abs muscles because he is going to be taking some shots there. Try not to kick him in the balls though as there is no way to toughen up that area, unless you're a Shaolin Monk or something. Kicking there in the street is ok though.

Now that we have done some basic drills let's talk about one last thing you should be working on. The ever so forgotten super secret technique and a technique that is usually not thought about even in the dojo. It's called PUNCHING. Everyone thinks they know how to punch until they get into a real fight and then what happens? They end up wearing a cast on their hand the next day. I've seen it so many times that I just want to start asking these guys, who taught them how to punch? And let me say something right now that might ruffle some feathers. If you can absolutely get away without throwing a punch with your fist in a fight then do it. What kind of bull crap is that you say? I would rather use elbows, open heel palm, hammer fist, or forearm strikes before I use my fist. It's just too easy in a real fight to hit something hard that will hurt your hand or not strike someone properly in the right place that will also injure your hand. It takes years and years of conditioning to be able to hit someone just about anywhere without getting hurt. And even then it's not guaranteed. I've seen guys that I've known to condition their hands and had all the calluses and everything come around with a cast on. When I ask them what happened it's usually the, I got into a fight and accidently caught the guys forehead. Will you be able to get away without using your fist in a fight? Maybe or maybe not. Just keep that in mind. So now that I've told you all that, let's take a look at how to hit someone with a regular fist the right way.

There are a couple solid ways to hit someone that I have used that didn't get anything in my hand damaged. One thing that I think needs to be said is what NOT to do. One would be to hit a hard target (examples are forehead, top of skull, etc) or to hit someone using your pinky knuckle. Yeah, all you Jeet Kune Do practitioners are going, why, we use the last three knuckles including the pinky knuckle when we punch. Well, because it's just too easy to damage that particular knuckle especially on a hard target. I have damaged this knuckle many times and it hurts and takes a long time to heal. So don't do it. Don't care what kind of iron fist you think you have, you will break your hand on someone's forehead or other hard target. I'm sure someone will come up with a way to do it with some super secret training or technique but remember, this chapter is about basic techniques. These are techniques that you should be able to do with little training.

Ok, so what's a proper punch look like? Let's start with the basic fist which is another thing that really isn't covered in a lot of dojo's. Put your hand in front of your face with the palm facing you. Fold all your fingers up tightly, leaving your thumb out, right into where the creases are that separates your upper and lower palm. Really dig them in to the point where you can't pull them up any farther.

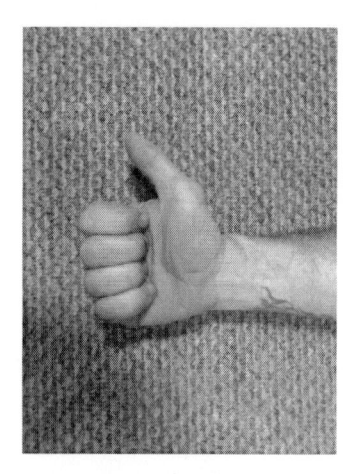

Now here is where you can do one of two things with your thumb. Either way you put your thumb it must be tight. You can fold your thumb onto the top of the index finger in between the middle knuckle and the knuckle that's close to the nail (not sure what the medical term for this is or if they're even medically called knuckles). Make sure that your thumbnail is not sticking out beyond the middle knuckle when you go to throw a punch. The other placement is to tuck your thumb into the side of the index finger at the crease below the middle knuckle. Your thumbnail should be pointing roughly into the crease but not wrapped up by the index finger. Don't wrap it up with the index finger because that's how you break your thumb. Your thumb should be digging into the crease and not extend anywhere outside of that crease when throwing a punch.

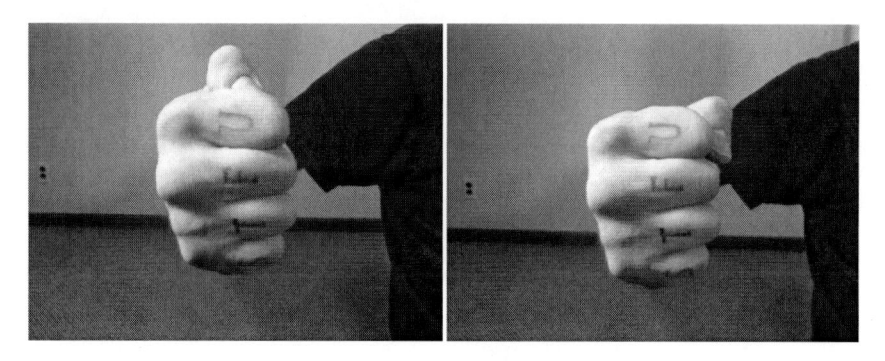

Is that it? No. Let's take a look at what part of the fist you're going to hit with. Here's another source of contention between different fighting styles. I will tell you what I use that hasn't messed up my hand. Anyone who knows me knows how much tape I use on my fingers when I go to the dojo and it is from getting injured over the years by punching the wrong way. And let me tell you, you can practice this stuff forever but still get injured in a fight because a fight is fast and the adrenaline will be soaring and sometimes it just happens that you don't do this or that while in the heat of battle. It is what it is but the more practice you have the more chance of you mitigating those risks. I use my index and middle finger knuckles to hit with. The ring finger knuckle is ok too but it can get too close to the pinky knuckle for comfort.

Ok, so is that it? Nope, not yet. Looking at this as I'm writing, I might have been able to almost write a whole chapter about punching. Anyway, the next thing is the wrist. There must be a straight line between the knuckles you're hitting with and your wrist. Sometimes when you look at this it can look cockeyed but it's really not. The straight line will be internal and not on the top of your skin. You don't want you wrist to bend when you hit something. If it bends it will hurt and this injury sucks. Trust me, I have had this happen more than a few times. Usually when hitting the heavy bag. Why? Because I got lazy with my technique. Remember that from another chapter? Yes, it has bit me in the ass a few times too. No one is perfect.

Now for stances. What should you use? Anything you feel comfortable with and can avoid and maneuver out of most hits that are coming for you. If you can work out of all the stances then outstanding. I practice rotating between all of them. Standard stance (right handed), Southpaw stance (for lefties), Square stance (more like a Muay Thai stance), Back stance (more of a baiting stance where most of the weight is on the back foot with the other foot in front of you). Just remember that the important point of all the stances and moving around in them is that you remain balanced and when you hit or kick you must be grounded. So don't be bouncing around like an idiot but make sure to keep everything moving, including your hands and arms, while still keeping the three most important things in mind. I used to yell this to my kids all the time when they were training. Hands up, elbows in, chin tucked.

Below pictured as the standard stance, southpaw stance, square stance, and the back stance:

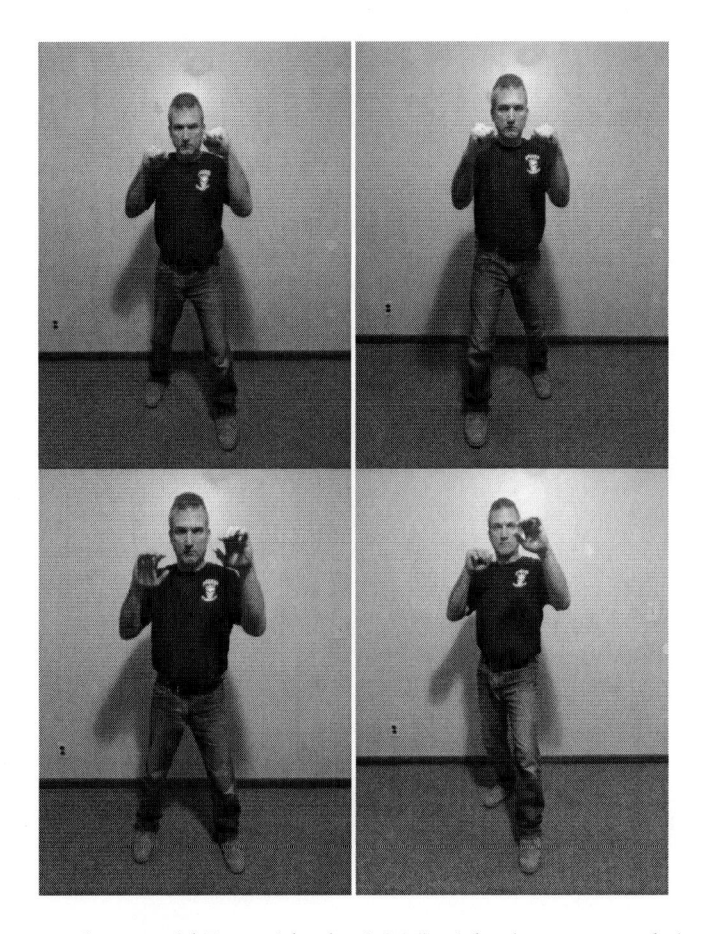

So what punches would I consider basic? The jab, the cross, and the hook. Yes there is an uppercut but the other three are what you will mostly see in an altercation. Well, that is, from someone who doesn't know what they are doing. You will also see a whole bunch of haymakers, which are basically highly telegraphed hook punches, being thrown in an altercation. But as far as the uppercut goes, it takes a little more time to master the upper cut to do it correctly and it's a very short range punch.

For the jab, let's start in the standard stance. You can use whatever stance you like but will have to modify which hand is going to do the jab depending on the stance you're using. So in the stance you're comfortable with, take the hand that is in front and with a proper fist and all the other tips as described in this chapter, shoot it straight out, while rotating your palm to face down, and after it hits the target, bring it back in as fast as you can. You don't want to lunge out, you want to keep your body solid and centered. Don't clench your fist until right before you hit the target. This keeps you arm loose so it can be as fast as possible. Make sure you keep your other hand up to protect your head. It's usually not a power punch but it can be if you work on it. In a real fight it can be used as a distraction, a punch to the face, or to push someone back. Jabs are usually followed by the cross or hook punches. There are all kinds of ways to do a jab but most of them are for the ring and not the street. That in a nutshell is a jab.

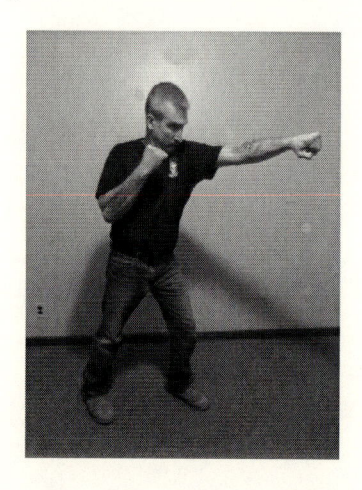

Now the cross, the punch you see right after a couple of jabs, is your power punch. Don't just throw the cross out there without intention because unlike the jab, if you miss you're exposing your now forward moving face toward your opponent. If you miss you're going to want to get your hands back up as fast as possible. You don't have to throw knockout power crosses all day but make sure the ones you do throw out there count. A lot of energy is expended by crosses.

A proper cross will be made with whichever hand is in the rear. So if your left foot is forward (standard stance) your cross would be made with the right hand. Once again, with all the other tips in this chapter in mind, throw your rear hand out while rotating your palm down. Extend your arm out and distribute your weight from the rear foot to your lead foot. This is accomplished by pivoting on the ball of your rear foot, rotating your body like in a whipping motion, and bending your knees and leaning forward slightly but not too much. All this should be done at the exact same time as the cross is thrown. When you pivot on the ball of your foot make sure you don't lift your whole foot off the ground but go up on your toes and pivot on them. Almost like you're putting out a cigarette on the ground with your toes. Bring your hand back as fast as possible because again, if you miss, you could be exposing yourself to all kinds of counter punches. Make sure your opponent is actually in your range so you don't have to over extend to reach him. I see this kind of cross all the time. Usually the guy does some kind of goofy looking sneaky cross. Like actually bending way down and launching his cross out there with his outside shoulder facing directly at his opponent. This is the "I don't want to get hit" way of throwing punches. Problem with that is when you have to fight someone who knows even just a little bit about fighting. They will catch on to this quickly and tag you plus it also has no power behind it. So that's the cross.

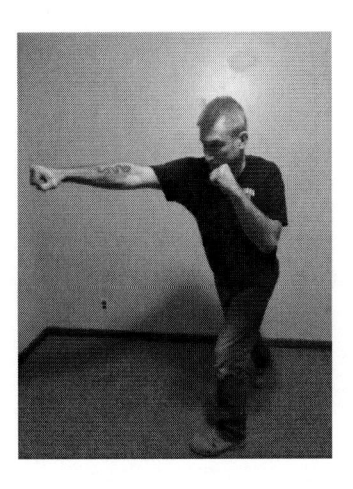

So now let's move on to the hook punch. The hook punch is where most knockouts are seen both in the ring and on the street. You will most likely see the haymaker on the street which is a highly telegraphed hook but they can still knock you out. You can throw a hook with your lead hand or your rear hand. So with all the other tips in mind, when you throw the hook, bend your arm at about a 90 degree angle and then rotate your body while throwing the punch. You will also be pivoting on the ball of your foot as you're throwing the hook. Whichever hand you're throwing the hook with, that same side foot will do the pivoting. Make sure you're bending your knees slightly while still maintaining balance and then try to follow through with the punch so that you get the most power from it. Make sure that if you miss you get that hand back immediately. Because with the hook, if you miss badly you have a very good chance of getting knocked out yourself with the dreaded haymaker that all the drunks like to throw over and over and over again. Anyway, the target for the hook is usually the side of the jaw or my favorite place to strike, the side of the neck right below the jaw line. Remember what I said? Soft targets are better for your knuckles. You can also hit anywhere on the side of the body. Maybe target the liver or outside rib areas.

BASIC TECHNIQUES

A good way to practice punching is the good old heavy canvas bags as they're great for punching, kicking, knees, elbows, head or whatever. They last forever and they will start to roughen up your knuckles and condition them better than any other bag. That is if you use them with bare knuckles. Some of the other bags I have used are the water bags, which are good and solid but they're way more forgiving than the canvas bags. I'm not saying they're bad because I use them too. They just won't give you the feedback if you make a bad punch that the canvas bags will. Yeah, I'm talking about hurting your hand on the canvas bag if you do something wrong. Hey, if you don't know what it feels like to hurt your hand when making a bad punch and then work on NOT making a bad punch, then when it does happen in a real fight you will most likely get your ass kicked because you will have unfamiliar pain and probably ease up or get distracted. I remember as a kid I always wanted to touch the inside of the oven door when my Mom opened it after cooking something. Why? Who the hells knows. My Mom kept on yelling at me to not touch it. One day my Grandmother was there and said, let him touch it. He won't learn to not touch it if he isn't familiar with the pain associated with touching it. Well, I touched it and guess what. Oh yeah, I got burned, but to this day I have never burned myself on the inside of an oven door again. That's teaching someone a lesson old school. What does that have to do with anything? The more pain you feel when doing something wrong the more apt you are to not do it wrong when it counts. Why do you think this whole chapter seems like it's all about you taking an ass beating? Because that's the point. The more you can take and are familiar with the better off you will be in a real altercation. You will have less of the "what the hell was that" moments and you will be able to focus more on what you have to do to fight back.

Up until this point we have talked about all the things you will need to do to prepare for a fight. Basic stuff that will get you by and give you an understanding of fighting and taking a beating while getting used to getting hit. But I know someone is going to ask about specific techniques they can use in a fight. Well most of them that I like to use will be in the Advance chapter because you will need a little more training than taking hits and hitting stuff. But let's say there are a few that can be done quite effectively without a lot of training. One of my favorites is called the Brachial Stun.

So before I tell you what it is and how to, in my opinion, properly use it, I want to say that most karate guys are going to get upset with what I am about to say.

So first, to explain what that is, a brachial stun is a sharp blow to the side of the neck that can cause unconsciousness by shock to the carotid artery, jugular vein, and vagus nerve. An even more basic definition would be to say it's a strike to the side of the neck.

How do you do this in a fight? Well first, you need to have worked on all the other stuff mentioned in this chapter because if you can't get in to make a hit, you're wasting your time. You will probably get hit at some point during an altercation. You will want to strike the side of the neck and focus on hitting below and slightly in front of the ear. What do you hit the neck with? Well you have probably seen it in the dojo with someone showing you a "karate chop" strike with the outside of their hand. And it's usually shown in a quick chopping motion where they strike really fast and take it away really fast. Here is where someone is going to get mad at me. THIS WONT WORK 90 percent of the time. Why? Because the person who you're fighting isn't just going to be standing there and let you hit him with a dojo style karate chop. They're going to be moving as well. Striking in this way is low percentage at best and there is a good chance that you will injure your hand.

The best way to use this technique is with the inside or outside of your forearm with a downward strike while driving it into him. In using your forearm, you will need to be a little closer than regular striking range. Maybe a bull rush strike or while in the clinch would be a good way to execute this. If you use the inside of your forearm then it would sorta look like a hook punch but with your arm a lot more extended and if you used the outside of your forearm it would look like a back fist strike. This strike needs to be driven into the neck and with as much force as you can get. The downward angle will make sure you're hitting all the areas that need to be hit to actually take him down.

BASIC TECHNIQUES

And yes, you're probably going to get hit. I keep on saying this because there is no winner in any fight. More often than not, you will have some injury as well even if you knocked the crap out of whomever you were fighting. Just keep that in mind. That's why I wrote all the other chapters first because recognizing a potential fight coming and getting away from it is better than actually getting into a fight. Especially the older and older you get.

Ok, so now that we talked about that, I have one more technique, or group of techniques that I love to use that will get someone to let go of you and back them up almost instantly. It won't put them down for good by any means but it will give you a chance to get away. I say group of techniques because they are just places to strike that are high percentage. There are a ton of places to strike but a lot of them you can miss and just piss off whoever just attacked you. You don't want this. It will just make the situation worse for you. These techniques are used for getting the hell out of there. Ok?

I'm not going to go into detail on them because they really don't need much explaining. Well, maybe except for the first one. I like to call it the neck claw. I use my index and middle finger and put them together tightly at an extended but slightly bent angle like a claw. Now drive these fingers into the front middle of the neck right below the adams apple and where the two collar bones come together. Should feel like a little pit that has hard bone around it and soft in the middle. Now as you're pushing your fingers into that area start driving down in a hooking motion like you are trying to insert you fingers deep into his esophagus. Keep on pushing in and down until they let go. If you're doing it correctly they will let go and start coughing and probably have water in their eyes. Now remember, RUN.

You can try this in the dojo but go slowly.

Here are some more time tested techniques.

Knee to the testicles. I like the knee because it is very high percentage and will do some damage even if you miss. Striking with your hand or foot is good but it tends to be on the lower percentage and you will have just given away what you're intending to do. They will protect that area immediately after a missed strike. I want to say something about the knee strike because I see a lot of dojo's teaching the knee strike incorrectly. The correct way to knee someone no matter where you strike them is to keep your toes pointed down when raising your knee up while slightly leaning back. This produces the most amount of force as you're driving that knee into hm.

BASIC TECHNIQUES

If I mentioned the testicle strike then I might as well mention the eye rake. I don't really like this one too much because unless you hit the eyes dead on you just going to just piss him off. And I've been accidently hit in the eyes in the dojo and I know I could recover very quickly and continue to fight. I believe it's just a low percentage technique. I just had to mention it because it's taught in every dojo I've been to. A better way to use it in my opinion would be to cover up his eyes by placing your hand and mainly fingers over his eyes. Start pushing your fingers into his eyes and feeling around while trying to get into them into his eye sockets. At the very least he will close his eyes so you can follow up with a higher percentage distraction and make him let go. I don't really like the eye rake but it's so prevalent in dojo's and women's self defense classes that I had to at least give a more high percentage way to do it. Take it for what it is and make it yours.

A more high percentage strike that I would use would be the ear clap or nose bop.

The ear clap is just as it sounds. You can use one hand or two. Make your hand into an open cup while your fingers are all tightly together and slightly bent. Now take that hand and bash it into the ear. It creates pressure in the ear and will defiantly do some damage. It's a strike to stun and distract.

The nose bop you will use the lower palm of your hand and smash it into the nose area. You can angle it from below or right into the nose or even sideways. What's great about this one is that you will do damage even if you miss your exact target. Even grazing the nose will cause his eyes to water and some sharp pain. And again, after that strike or any of the other strikes lands, RUN.

There are hundreds of techniques out there and some of them work and some of them don't. The more you train the more some of them might work. I want to give you techniques that I know work and then you can see what else works for you while training. Always think and take everything with a grain of salt. The more you make a technique into instinct the more of a chance you will have if something does go down for real. You will have to adapt quickly to every situation as no situation really ever goes the way you think it should go. That's just the cold hard truth.

BASIC TECHNIQUES

So in saying all that, please keep in mind that all the basic techniques, while basic, are dangerous. You should not take them lightly. Pretty much this whole book has hopefully now gotten you to think about NOT taking things lightly. Wear protective equipment as you think you need it. If you want to scale down on protective equipment at your pace then scale down at your pace. Only take as much as you can handle. Strive for personal bests. These are not techniques that you do just because you have nothing better to do. These are techniques to train like a warrior but have fun doing it. Yes, I said it. As much of a psycho that I may seem to be, I do know that you have to have fun when training for the long haul. So train on.

9 ADVANCED TECHNIQUES

So now that we have gone over a bunch of basic stuff lets now move on to the advanced stuff. If you're looking for some secret magic technique then you will be disappointed. There is no such thing. I see all over the internet guys talking about how their style of fighting techniques are the best and sometimes when I watch some of these videos I just have to ask if they have ever been in a real fight. There is some real garbage out there that looks really cool but will never work as it's presented.

What do I have and use that I call advanced? Well, none of my advanced techniques are very pretty or cool looking. They just work and are really multiple basic techniques, for the most part, just strung together. I don't like to mess around with techniques that require a lot of fine motor skills because it takes a long long time to convert fine motor techniques into techniques that can be used like gross motor techniques. What do I mean by this? Fine motor techniques are techniques that incorporate the coordination of small muscles when moving and usually involve the synchronization of the hands and fingers with the eyes. In other words, they're techniques that require a lot of dexterity and calmness when trying to execute them. During a fight we have the problem of adrenaline exploding inside us that will take away a lot of that dexterity and most if not all of the calmness. Hence, in order to pull off any kind of fine motor technique you have to be in complete control of yourself and be calm. You know, mind like water? It takes a long time to actually get to this level if ever. I've been training in martial arts for a long time and I still have trouble with this one sometimes.

Ok then, so what are gross motor techniques and why are they better? Gross motor techniques are techniques that use the large muscles in our bodies like the torso, arms and legs to complete whole body movements. So to put it plainly, they're techniques that don't take a lot of coordination or calmness to pull off. Hell, you could be piss drunk and still be able to smash someone in the face with a forearm right? Not saying that you wouldn't get your ass kicked afterwards but that's what gross motor techniques are.

So that's the difference between fine motor techniques and gross motor techniques. My advanced techniques are mostly gross motor techniques along with some fine motor techniques that I believe can be learned and engrained in the gross motor technique column with a relatively short amount of training. What do I mean by relatively short? Well, you WILL need to train them over and over again a couple hundred times but it's a lot shorter time than some of the other more fancy, pretty, or cool looking techniques that I have seen out there.

And since I keep on bringing up the pretty or cool looking stuff I just have to bring up some examples in the martial art Aikido. Now before I say anything that will ruffle some feathers, I just want to say that I have trained in Aikido for many years. It is one of my favorite martial arts. The big debate that I usually hear is will it work on the street? My answer is, it depends. I am not going to go into a philosophical debate on the different styles of Aikido and which ones are the best. I have been to so many Aikido dojo's over the years and have seen some really good stuff and some really useless stuff. Most of Aikido uses fine motor techniques. That's why when people start taking Aikido they think they can kick everyone's ass and then they find out the hard way that they can't. Then they quit. The first problem with Aikido is that most dojo's don't pressure test their techniques. That means they don't test the techniques using a fully or mostly fully resisting partner. They usually just punch and leave their whole arm sticking out there for the taking. That's ridiculous and won't teach you anything about actually using the technique in a real fight.

The second problem is that most Aikido styles don't incorporate striking. The dojo I trained in Aikido always said to strike first, during, and after the technique but really didn't make it a priority to push that it. And even when they did push the striking as some sensei's did, they didn't push striking the correct way and the correct places. Just because you slap someone lightly across the face doesn't mean you're going to distract that person every time. You might just piss him off even more and make him hold on tighter or come after you harder.

So let me get off bashing Aikido because it's an awesome martial art and can absolutely be used in a fight if done correctly. Are all my advanced techniques based on Aikido? No. In my opinion, it takes way too long to become proficient at Aikido to use it in a real fight. There are a few techniques that can be incorporated in this advanced technique chapter that can be trained into your muscle memory in a relatively short amount of time though. Remember my explanation of the words relatively short and take that into consideration.

The first technique that I use a lot is a technique that can be used to defend against that pesky haymaker punch. This one I see all the time in bar fights and street brawls. It's easy to see it coming but can still hurt you badly if you don't react quickly. I like techniques that incorporate moving forward into an opponent. I always tell students to not back up and give up ground. If you let someone back you up they will eventually have the momentum and barrel you over. There is a time to back up but don't do it for very long. Maybe only once. So once you see that haymaker coming, and you should have been aware of what was going on around you if you read all the previous chapters right, you need to get your hands up immediately. Before that haymaker gets too far you need to rush in with your hands up as if you were carrying a soccer ball about two feet in front of your face. Keep your arms slightly bent and make contact with your arm that is closest his body and slam that anywhere in between his shoulder and the middle of his bicep. Your other arm should slam simultaneously into the middle of his forearm. You should be making contact with the middle of your forearm while still moving toward him. This should, if done correctly and with the proper intent (as I spoke about in a previous chapter) stop or greatly inhibit his momentum.

Immediately following contact, guess what is right near his open face? Yup, your elbow. With intent, slam your elbow into the middle of his face. Done

ADVANCED TECHNIQUES

yet? No. I told you a lot of my advanced techniques are multiple basic techniques strung together. Just like combinations. So now, if slamming an elbow into his face once is good then three times should be even better right? Yup. But the last two make sure you take your other now available hand and grab the back of his head like in the clinch drills. Bring his head into your elbow as you're firing away. Done with him? Nope. This guy was pretty aggressive with you to begin with and didn't leave you any way out of the situation right? Ok then, since you already have him in a one handed clinch make it a two handed clinch and slam his head into a table or wall. If none around then lift your knee up while leaning slightly back and pointing the toes down and bring his head into your knee. If his head is way too far back slam your knee into his mid section. The knee strike can also be done multiple times. I'm fond of the number three. If he's still in a fighting mood after that he is on drugs or something and you should get the hell out of there. If you made contact with intent a number of times and he is not on some psycho drug, he will be on the floor. Warning, hitting someone with an elbow and knee multiple times in the face will most likely produce a lot of blood. Do not freak out. Calm down and assess the situation immediately. Are there other attackers around? Go back into hypervigilant mode and pay attention to everything around you while getting out of there.

Remember, if you paid attention to all the previous chapters and used that information you wouldn't be in this situation to begin with. So once the danger has been neutralized and the guy is on the ground, get out of there. Don't wait for his friends to come around. I know a lot of people teach so called techniques for taking on multiple attackers but let me tell you one thing right now. They're full of crap. It's a gamble to take on one person let alone multiple attackers. Even if you're the greatest martial artist in the land it doesn't guarantee that you have seen everything and won't get hurt while defending yourself. All techniques I have seen to fight multiple attackers try to line up the attackers so that you only fight one at a time. Problem with that is that it's not so easy to fight one person while trying to keep the others off you. They will shortly over run you. It's one thing to run around a big open dojo and fend off multiple attackers but how about a small bar room? That's where you will see the brawl fights with multiple people right? Trust me, you will get hit and you will get hit a lot in these situations. The victors, not that anyone gets out of a fight unscathed, usually have the numbers. The more fighters you have with you the more likely you are to come out on top. So my point is that trying to fight multiple attackers should be left for the movies.

Ok, so what's next in the advanced techniques? Well, if we just did the good old haymaker, what about the jab or cross punches? I like techniques that you can use against multiple attacks. This one is no different. It's the parry block sequence. At least that's what most people call it. The way I see it it's more of a parry, parry, sticky fingers technique. Because if you're going to parry someone you don't want to keep on doing that all day. If there is a chance to grab someone then do it and don't give up whatever you just grabbed.

Actually this technique could be used against the haymaker too as well as just about any other punch. The reason I really like this technique is that even if you screw it up by going with the wrong hand you will still be in a good position to defend yourself. You will either end up on the inside or outside and still be able to follow-up with something.

In basic terms, the way it is carried out is as follows. Say someone is throwing a punch at you with their right hand. You would take your right hand and wave it across your body, like you're swatting a fly, towards his punching arm. The bend and height of your arm is exactly the same as in the last technique. Hands up like you're carrying a soccer ball about two feet from your face with your arms slightly bent. The other hand should be coming up and under your right arm. Your right hand will then make contact with his right punch and perry it, not to be confused with blocking. A perry is just a slight redirection. You don't want to block it out of the way because you're going to use your other hand to perry it as well and then grab a hold of it. So as you perry with your right hand your left hand should be coming up right underneath your right arm and parrying his punch right about the same place as your first perry. But this time, with your left hand once you perry wrap your fingers and hand around his punching arm like you have a monkey's hand. You know, like using your fingers and thumb to grab over the top of his arm. You now have his arm and are on the inside. I

ADVANCED TECHNIQUES

say perry-perry-sticky fingers as opposed to perry-grab like some teach it because usually a student will try to perry and then grab right away like they're trying to catch the punch. You're not going to catch a punch.

So now what do you do after you have his arm? Well just don't sit there and think you just mesmerized him with your prowess. He is going to realize this and immediately try to hit you with the other hand. You don't have time to spare especially on the inside which is where you are now. Once you're done with all the parrying and grabbing you need to immediately, and I mean immediately, hit him. Well, since we are on the inside now and in close just as with the haymaker, what do you think we should use? Sure, elbows to the face. And several times I might add. Once you have his arm and the advantage, do not give it up. Be relentless and put him down. Then get the hell out of there right? Right. Good, you were listening.

So what was I talking about when I said you would end up in a good position even if you screwed it up? Well let's say that same strike came in with him trying to hit you with his right hand. Now this time you use your other hand, left, and bring that across your body to perry his punch to your right side. Then your right hand comes under your left and does another perry and sticky finger grab and "wa la", you're on the outside now. Even better right? Now you have his arm in front of you while standing behind it. Wow, what can we do from here? I love elbows so let's just end it here. Drop your elbow down on his outstretched elbow effectively breaking it in half. Might hear some popping or crunching but the fight will most likely be over. Yes, and again, get out of there.

This is a great technique that can be practiced anywhere. It's almost like you can sit there and practice your circles all day as that's what it look like when you practice it alone. The contact from each hand upon your attackers arm should be almost simultaneous and fast. Your counter strike should be immediate as well. Now some people will say if it's so good why don't boxers use it? Well they do to some extent. Look it up. The difference is that they're wearing big GLOVES and are going round for round. I'm not trying to teach you boxing I'm trying to show you how to fight if you have to. And fighting because you have to doesn't mean going punch for punch with your hands up and running around a ring. You want to be done with a fight as quickly as possible and get the hell out of there. The longer you spend going toe to toe with someone the more the chance of you getting hurt badly go up exponentially.

Now that you have some defense and follow-ups for strikes how about something for when you get in close as in when someone grabs you and wants to take you down. These are usually guys who are drunk and gas out quickly or some sleaze bag who wants to take down a female to rape her. Well good thing about someone grabbing you like that is their arms are now useless to them and aren't a threat to you. Yes they're grabbing on to you and hugging you but they won't be able to hit you. Just be careful of their knees and where they are. Don't forget about the head butt as well.

This is one of my favorite take down techniques other than foot sweeps because it's fairly easy to do and it can also be screwed up and still work to some degree. The technique is called major outer reap or O Soto Gari for you Judo guys. If you know Judo, the same way we do the major outer reap in Judo can also be used, exactly as taught in Judo, on the street. If you've never been to a Judo class then let me explain what it is and how you can do it.

Stand in front of someone and take your left hand and grab their right arm at the elbow right at the bend. Take your other hand and grab their shirt on their left side right below the collarbone. If you were both wearing a gi then this would be the same way we do it in Judo. However, we don't have gi's and this is not Judo. Now move in with your right shoulder making its way toward his right shoulder/chest area. Take his right arm that you were holding and start to wrap it up under your arm, as if you were chicken winging his arm, and pull him down and to the side in that direction to break his balance. Take your other hand that is grabbing his shirt and pull it up into his face as if you were trying to punch him in the face with an uppercut. As you're slamming into him take your left foot and step to his right side parallel with his foot or even beyond his foot for even more leverage. It can't be too close to his right foot because you still have to get your other foot in between. Then take your right leg and swing it around his right side beyond his leg and then sweep it back taking his right leg with it. This is all done while driving into him as he is off balance sideways and backwards. If done correctly he will end up on the ground with you standing over him holding onto his right arm. That's the way to do major outer reap with street clothes on. There are a ton of different variants to this and ways to pull it off. Just ask anyone who practices Judo and they will tell you. Get good at this and you will be surprised how easy it is to pull off.

Now, the way I just described the major outer reaping is how to learn it. How to actually pull it off while someone is wrapping you up is another. You must first get some distance between you and the person who is wrapping you up. Best way to do that is to hit him, elbow him, or if your arms are also wrapped up then push off or knee him in the groin. Whatever it takes to make some space. Once you have that space the next most important thing is to get him off balance. You can't throw someone who is not off balance. That's why smashing into him with your shoulder is one of the things that will take away his balance. What's good about this technique is it can also be used as a follow-up to all the previous techniques. Remember the haymaker and straight punches that we talked about? This can be done right after you block or parry those punches as you will be in perfect position to throw someone with major outer reaping.

Another really good way to take someone down with this is when you're wrapped up in close proximity to them. Maybe like two guys bear hugging

ADVANCED TECHNIQUES

each other in order to get the best position. All you have to think about is getting that one leg behind theirs and then pull them over your hip. The deeper you get you leg the better. If you can actually get half of your butt behind theirs then even better. Just make sure you're driving forward and not over stretching or leaning backwards to get there. Then you will be off balance and guess what the counter to major outer reaping is? Another major outer reaping. I've pulled the counter off more than I have the actual initial reap. Sometimes I bait someone to go for the major outer reap just to counter it with my own reap. The counter is easy. Just step back and maybe if you have to, a little sideways, and you're already in position to throw your own.

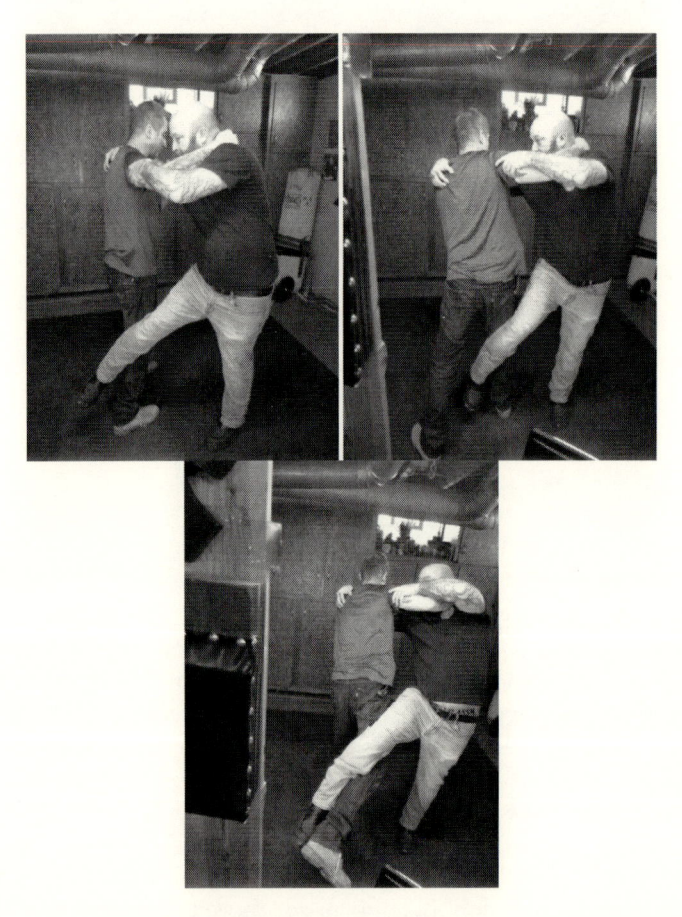

Can you see my path here yet? I like techniques that you can use in just about any situation. It's great to learn a whole ton of really cool complex and flashy techniques but the problem is when you actually try to pull them off. If you've practiced a thousand techniques a few times how are you going to recall that technique in a violent crazy fast situation where your adrenaline and fear are super high? You're not. It's better to practice a few techniques a thousand times so that it will almost be instinct when you have to pull it off for real.

So is going to a dojo and learning all kinds of different stuff a waste of time? Hell no. It's great to see all kinds of different techniques because you never know who will try some of them on you. The more you're aware of the more you can defend against. Plus, like I said before, I've paid a price for having a one tract view of the world and how evil it is. My kids used to say that all I talk about is the evil out there and how to defend against it. I wish I could have just had fun practicing martial arts with my kids and just have been a regular dad to them and friends with the people I met along the way. I'm starting to learn that now but this book was about giving back and I'm trying to tell you that there's more out there than evil. Martial arts are a great way to have a lot of fun and stay in awesome shape and make some really good friends. And some of the friends I finally made I call my brothers and sisters. That reference was only reserved for friends I had who were actually in the military up until recently. I don't use the term brother or sister lightly.

I mentioned in the last technique that it was one of my favorite techniques after foot sweeps. Foot sweeps are great for putting someone down quickly and still controlling your own balance and remaining upright. Foot sweeps are great because there are a ton of different ways to carry them out. Just ask anyone who takes Judo. Foot sweeps use the other guy's momentum against him. I know a lot of people hear this and say, yeah that's great in practice but how about real life? They're perfect for real life situations as well. Remember in school being tripped by the school bully? Well tripping is a form of foot sweep. It's pretty much a foot sweep by definition. A foot sweep is anything that will block the way the foot is traveling, like a trip, or making the foot move farther than it was intended to move. The last one is like someone yanking the chair out from underneath you as you're going to sit down. Guess what usually happens? You land square on your ass. Well if someone is moving their foot forward to take a step and you take your own foot and move their foot farther than they were expecting to move theirs guess what happens? Yup, they do a weird split and land on their ass. A foot sweep is perfect for that drunk guy who grabs on to you and wants to fight. Moving these guys to a position to foot sweep them is easy. A lot of the time they will be taking weird awkward exaggerated steps and are already off balance because they're drunk.

My favorite way to pull this one of is when someone grabs me. I usually go into a close hold, either clinch or grabbing their arms and shoulder, and then get them going sideways. You can then stick your own foot out to stop their foot from going sideways and they proceed to fall down while you still have control of their arm. Even if it doesn't work and they regain their balance it's a great time to strike them with a fist or elbow. When someone is that off balance, even if they don't fall down, they can't protect themselves.

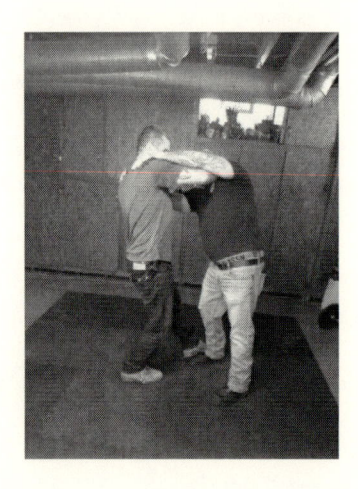

Another good point about foot sweeps is that on the street we are all wearing shoes. I wear construction boots so that's even better. When someone gets hit with a boot to their ankles, it hurts. So that's why even if they don't go down from your attempted foot sweep they will be off balance and now they have to deal with the pain in their ankles. Foot sweeps are good for distractions as well because of this point. Hurt someone down below and they won't be thinking up top. Hurt someone up top and they won't be thinking down below. Get where I'm going with this?

What are you doing with your upper body while trying to pull off a foot sweep? You will be using your arms to move them in the direction that they're going to be falling. So if you're moving them to your left and then you take your left foot and stop their right foot from moving, as in a trip, then you will be taking your arms and hand on whatever you're grabbing and steer them in that direction. When they fall just don't let go. Why? Because you already have a hold of them. Why would you let a perfectly good hold go? You will have at least one of their arms. Start wailing away in their neck area or underarm.

Another way to foot sweep would be to get them moving backward or forward and then push or pull their foot farther than they were planning on stepping. And down they will go.

So there is the foot sweep for you. Come up with ways that work for you. They can be a little complicated in the beginning but once you get how to move they will be an awesome addition to have in your tool box.

I mentioned Aikido earlier in this chapter and I just have to put something in the advanced chapter that is an Aikido technique. I want to explain an Aikido technique that I know works on the street. Cops use it and so do bouncers. In Aikido it's called Ikkyo or first pinning/teaching. It is considered the most basic of all Aikido techniques and is used as an entrance for a ton of other Aikido techniques.

One caveat on this. Do not think you will pull this off without some kind of strike or distraction before you do the technique. Remember what I said before about Aikido? Striking first is imperative to pull off any kind of Aikido technique. This, I do not believe, is being stressed in most Aikido dojo's.

Anyway, how it is usually taught is that someone grabs your wrist and then you do an Ikkyo from there. Ok, great. First off, if you're a guy, I have never seen any fight that started with a guy grabbing another guy's wrist. That's usually reserved for some asshole boyfriend pulling his girlfriend back to the car or some low life trying to drag a kid into his van. I will touch on those examples but I will start with the more likely scenario of someone grabbing your shirt at the collarbone area with one hand or both hands. Better that they grab you with both hands because then they can't punch you without letting go.

Great, someone just grabbed you like this and shoved you up against a wall and are screaming all kinds of nonsense at you like what normally happens. Like I said, trying to do an Ikkyo right here and now isn't going to work because they're focusing all their strength on gripping your shirt and holding you against the wall. Well if he has his hands on you guess what's wide open? His balls. Knee to the privates should be a good distraction. Now take your opposite hand from his and pin his hand strongly into your shoulder. Pivot your whole body to the side keeping your hand on his hand in the center of your body as if a line were being drawn from the center of your face down to your abdomen. You will be using your shoulder and body as one to turn against his hand. Once you get him turned start peeling his hand over and then use your other hand to wrap around his elbow area. Your arms should be extended, again like carrying a soccer ball between them. You should now bring both of your hands, with his arm, down to your waist and pin it against your waist area. His shoulder should be lower than the hand you have a hold of. Walk forward and bring his arm to the ground pinning it there with both of your hands. I like to use my knee on his neck to further pin him down. Controlling the head at this point will effectively control his body.

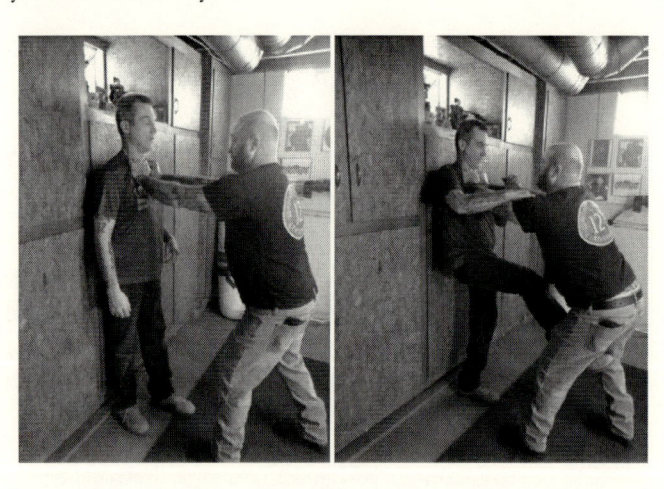

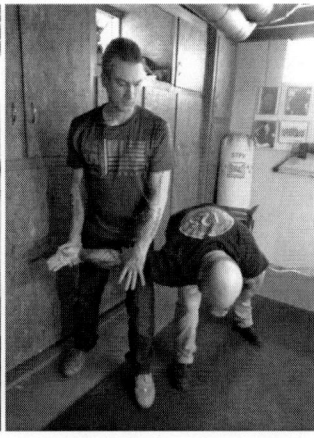

This technique can be a follow up to just about any strike block. You just have to practice getting your hands into the right places. Also make sure that these movements are not herky jerky. Aikido is all about flow and it does take a lot of practice to get some of this stuff down. That's why I only listed Ikkyo in my advanced techniques. There are others that I have used but it takes years and years to use them to any degree.

Now getting back to that one armed grab as if some jerk was grabbing his girlfriend. It doesn't matter what hand they grab you with but the way you would get your hands into place is a little different.

If someone grabs you with their left to your right hand, looks like a mirror image, then you would take your other free hand, place it on top of their hand that is grabbing you, peel it off and over while bringing it to your left side. Take your other hand that is now free and place it on their elbow of the hand you have. Then the rest is the same as in the last one. It's a little hard to grasp all the movements when you start but after a little while it should start to look pretty good. Hopefully the pictures give you a good idea on how to do this technique.

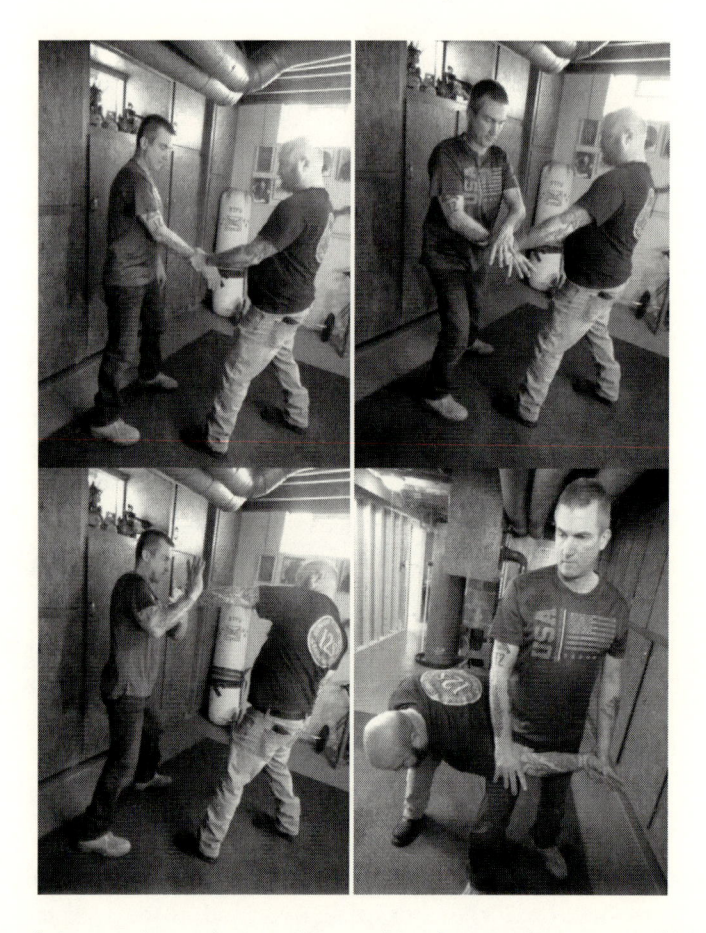

In one of the previous chapters I mentioned gun take away techniques. I want to say something before I write about gun takeaways. I was thinking about whether or not I should even write about them because even if you know what you're doing there is only about a 50 percent chance that it will work without you getting shot somewhere. And then after the take away you still have to deal with the guy that you just took his gun away from. Talk about gun retention after a takeaway and you're now dealing with a scenario that is absolutely life or death. So keep that in mind when training gun takeaways.

So why did I decide to write about gun takeaways? Because just about every dojo I have been to teaches them. And some are really hard to watch without me thinking about stepping in and saying what the hell are you teaching here? You're going to get someone killed.

I believe that gun takeaways are possible because I have seen them done for real. This is the one big caveat. You have to really assess the attacker's intent to know if you can get away with it or not. All the previous chapters apply here. If this guy has a gun and is pointing it at you and has any kind of intent to harm you if you make one move then the chances of you actually pulling a gun takeaway off goes way down. He will also come at you full bore if you do take it away from him. So if you don't think he is going to shoot you after you do whatever he says then just do what he says. If you think you're in imminent danger for your life then you gotta go for it and do what you need to do.

What's the first thing to do if you have assessed the situation and are convinced that you need to do something? Get out of the line of fire for one. I've seen too many times someone training will grab the gun while it's still pointed directly at them and THEN move out of the way. I will come over and say great, now you've just been shot. So the first thing is to get out of the way. I would rather go towards the outside than inside because if you do take away the gun at least you're on their outside and gained about a second where you can move away.

At the same time you're moving towards the side to get out of the line of fire, you will want to grab the gun by the barrel with BOTH HANDS and lift it up. I've heard all sorts of different ways to move the gun but don't forget there could be people standing behind you or to the side of you. Maybe your kids or wife. So up is the best bet. You don't have to lift it up as far as you can reach. Just slightly over your head is good. The angle that it will end up at will miss everyone standing on the ground if it's just above your head.

Once you have it raised up turn the barrel back into the attackers face by

ADVANCED TECHNIQUES

making his wrist bend in toward his inner forearm. It should be bent so much that it could snap his wrist or at least rip up some tendons. Up until this point, in Aikido, this technique is called kote gaeshi if anyone wanted to know. From there, with violent aggressive intent, smash the gun right into his teeth several times all while still holding the barrel with both hands. Will it go off during all of this? Probably. But if you're holding the barrel then it will only go off once because it won't be able to rack another round. Why? You're holding the part that does the reload and it won't be able to move. Unless it's a revolver and in that case just disregard everything about racking. Everything is still the same other than that.

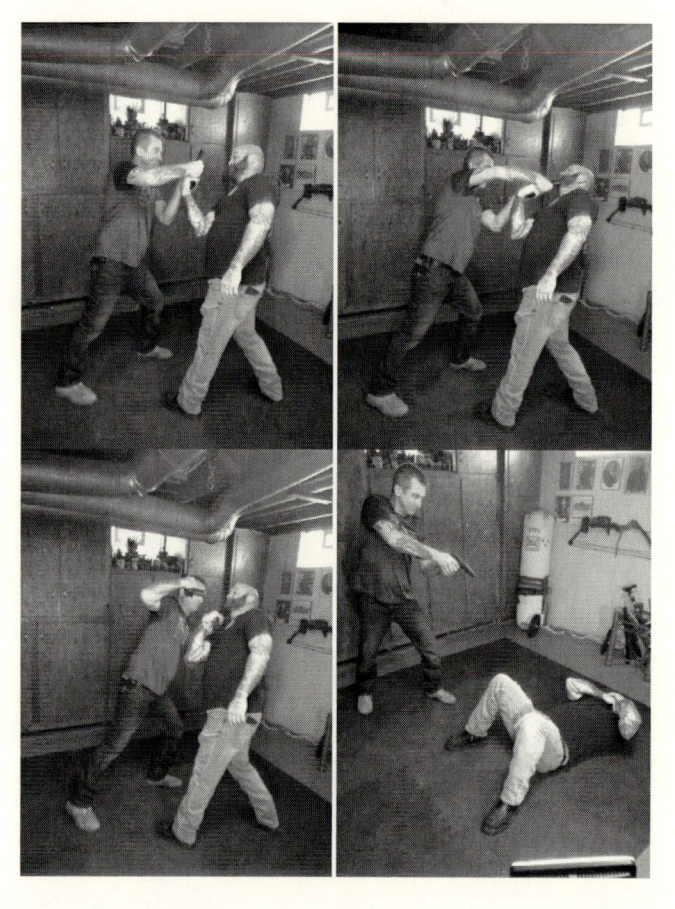

At this point he will have let go, the gun has probably gone off but hopefully it went off while it was pointed at his face. If not then that's ok just as long as it didn't hurt anyone standing around. And his mouth is probably gushing a ton of blood. Is it over? He might be on the ground with blood all over his face. If this is the case then back up, rack the gun and hold it on him. Call 911 or run like hell if there are any of his buddies around. Don't just drop the gun but keep it and get to a safe place and then call 911.

Ok so what if he didn't go down? I have seen this demonstrated in many dojo's and this is where the majority of them stop. One problem. IT'S NOT OVER. You think a guy that just tried to rob or kill you with a gun is going to stand there now that you have taken away his weapon? Hopefully for you, he just runs away. I don't think that will happen. He already had the balls to hold you up with a gun. This is next level stuff as opposed to someone trying to jack some old ladies purse. Odds say he is going to bum rush you to try to regain control of his weapon that you now have.

We are now in the gun retention realm. You have his gun and don't want him to take it back and must now defend yourself. You have a gun so no problem right? Not really. The first thing to assume is that if the gun already went off then maybe that was the only round in the magazine. If that was the case then the gun is still a good solid heavy piece of metal that you can hit him with. You just smashed him in the teeth with it. You've heard of pistol whipping right? Well use it like that.

So whatever way it came out of his hands and into yours you must now get it into your shooting hand so you can use it to put a bullet in him if possible. Once you get it there then bring it down to your side and face your opposite shoulder towards the attacker who is now coming at you hard. Make sure you rack the gun to chamber another round and then keep your other hand on top of the barrel holding the gun with both hands tightly. This way you can use the gun as a two handed bashing device. Make sure to point the barrel at the attacker while smashing it into his face or chest. This way you can take a shot and the gun will already be pointed at him.

ADVANCED TECHNIQUES

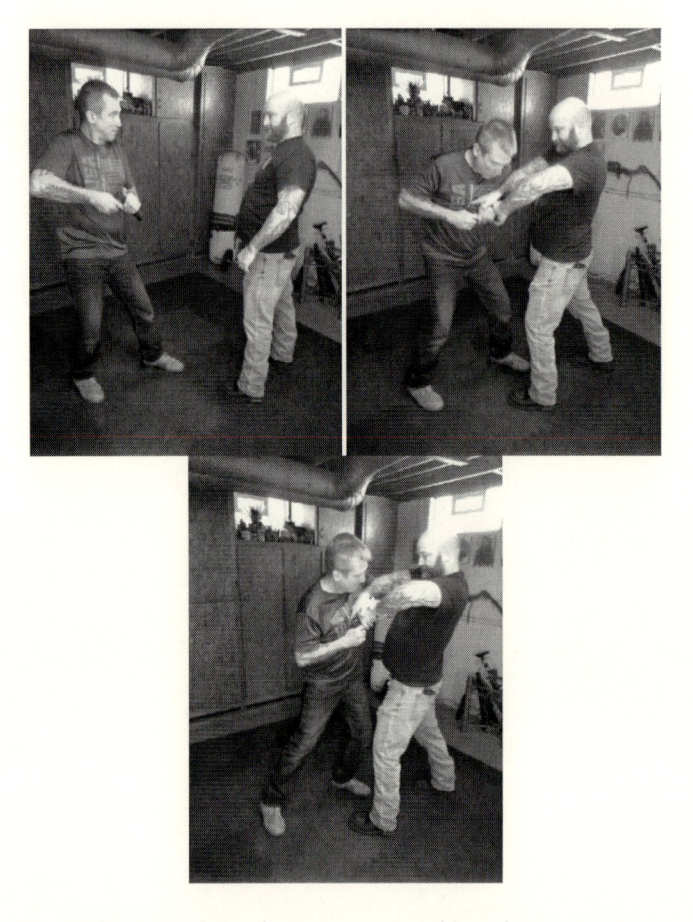

If you were paying attention when you were taking the gun away, your hand on the barrel now is pretty much used the same way here. So wont that allow only one shot to go off before you have to rack the gun again? Yes. If it goes off and your attacker doesn't go down then you will need to rack it again and perform the gun retention technique over again until your attacker drops. Keeping two hands on the gun and wrapped up at all times makes it very difficult to take the gun away from you while still giving you the opportunity to take shots on your target. And you need to put rounds in him if he is aggressively coming after you still. At the very least you still have a nice heavy piece of steel to bash him with if it has no more rounds left.

This is a thing many people don't realize. Just because you shoot someone doesn't mean they're going to drop to the ground and die instantly. That's mainly only in the movies. Unless you get a clean kill shot, the chances of you taking someone down with one shot when that person is bum rushing you are not good. Even with several on target shots he might still be able to come after you. He will eventually bleed out but don't think the fight is done until you see him lying on the ground not breathing. And just so you know, knife stabbings take even longer to kill someone unless they're done correctly. I have seen someone get stabbed at least a dozen times running around the street and then still get away. Don't know if he died later but he still had enough fight in him to get away. So my point is that even if something goes wrong and you get shot or stabbed, don't give up. Fight till you can't fight anymore and if you get away then get to a hospital immediately.

This technique can be used no matter what angle your attacker has his gun pointed at you. At your face, body, side, behind, doesn't matter. The most important thing to remember is to get off line and get a hold of the gun with both hands.

So I know I mentioned knife attacks. I know someone is asking about defending a knife attack. What's my technique for knife take aways? Run. God forbid someone attacks you with a knife and you have young kids around or someone who can't run. I have seen a ton of knife defenses but the percentage of getting out of a knife figth without getting really hacked up are worse than a defending yourself from a gun attack. A gun can kill you even if you're running away so yeah, if you think you're in grave danger then you gotta do what you gotta do. A knife can only hurt you if it makes physical contact with you. Hence, run away. All the knife defenses I have practiced or seen take a long long time to get right and I am really not sold on any of them. If you really thought that you had no other option than to fight a guy with a knife I would say that the same technique used for the gun takeaway would be your best bet. And even then it's really crappy odds. Just too much can go wrong with a knife. That's why I'd rather give you the RUN advice. Either that or just do what he says. Remember, even with a gun, if you don't think that the attacker will shoot you after you do whatever he says then DO WHAT HE SAYS.

My last technique might be a little controversial but this whole book is based on what a real situation can be and how to make it out alive to see another day. But I also don't want to see any of my readers to go to jail either. I will call the last technique Knuckles are Legal. What am I talking about? You might be thinking I'm talking about your own knuckles. I'm not. I am talking about brass knuckles. Stop and breath. Yes, brass knuckles. By the end of me explaining this I am going to convince you that carrying around brass knuckles is a good idea.

Now I know this goes way way deep into a big grey area so bear with me. Brass knuckles are an excellent carry weapon for women. Guys, you can carry them too but DO NOT take them out in some bar fight or any other situation where you might have been part of the cause. Yeah, I'm talking to you guys who drink way too much at the local bar and then shoot off your mouth at everyone who walks by you. Don't carry knuckles if you're this guy.

But what about the guy who works in a high risk area like being a contractor in a shitty neighborhood. Or any woman out there that wants something to carry and be able to use in a moment's notice. I'm hearing the "what about pepper spray" for us women? That's what a lot of you are carrying right? That's fine if it works correctly. Shooting someone with pepper spray, especially if you haven't practiced it, is a fine motor skill. You are using your finger to try to push that little button on top. Never mind the aiming it, making sure the spray comes out the right way, and hitting your target with it. What if he still gets a hold of you? You have your backup knuckles right? What about a gun you say? Sure. If you know how to use it and are willing to actually pull the trigger. You know, like the women whose husband went out and bought a gun for his wife to carry but the only training she has had was the pistol permit class and a couple times at the shooting range. Yeah, that one. If you're this person please don't carry. You're more likely going to have it taken away and used on you. My only advice is that the only time you should pull a gun is if you're going to shoot someone DEAD. Period. If you can't wrap your head around killing someone then don't bother carrying a gun. I'm not even going to go into what happens afterwards mentally. On top of all that, just ask a military vet or a cop what the ratio is of rounds fired to the ones that actually hit the intended target when in an altercation. The percentage is not a good one. And these are all highly trained individuals.

Ok, so now I've convinced you to carry knuckles and want to know which ones to carry. There are all sorts of different ones but I carry the standard boring knuckles. The ones that look like the original knuckles. I would advise against the ones with letters, spikes, and weird knuckle designs. Why? Because they will leave distinctive marks on someone who you just cracked across the forehead with them. Why would you care about that? The name of the chapter is Knuckles Are Legal right? Well, they are legal, until you get caught with them. At least where I live anyway. So if you're going to carry them then make sure you carry the ones that aren't going to leave a suspicious pattern on someone's forehead. And knuckles should be thought of the same as a knife or gun. You don't pull them out unless you absolutely have to. Knuckles can end an altercation very quickly if used correctly. But they can also do some damage quickly so don't use them unless you have to.

So how should knuckles feel in your hands to know they're the right ones for you? You should be able to get you whole fist around them while your fingers are inserted and be able to make a fist without having your fingers and hands not being able to fully grasp the knuckles. The holes, where you stick all your fingers, should be at the top of your knuckles with your fingers fully inserted and the bottom open grip of the knuckles should be wrapped up in your palm. The fist that you make with knuckles should be the same fist that I described how to make in the Basic Techniques chapter. You really want to hold on tight because you're using metal in lieu of your own knuckles. If you hold them too loosely you will damage your knuckles as the brass knuckles will come back into your own knuckles. A great way to test if you're holding them correctly with the right amount of grip is to hit a solid wall. If it hurts your own knuckles then hold onto the brass knuckles tighter. That's it.

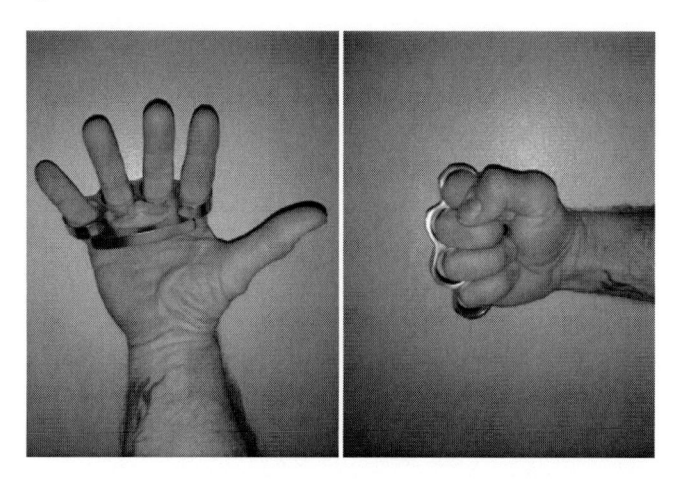

The great thing about knuckles is that they can be used to hit the places that

ADVANCED TECHNIQUES

we always inadvertently hit with our bare knuckles without meaning to. How any times have you been in a fight or seen a fight that someone ends up hurting their hand because they crack someone in the forehead. Yeah, quickest way to break your hand. Well those are the exact places you will be hitting with brass knuckles. Why? Because if you're wearing something as hard as brass knuckles you aim for the hard targets. Not soft targets like you would if hitting someone with bare knuckles. What are examples of hard targets? Anything that has bone directly under the skin. The forehead, top of head, elbows, knees, feet, hands are all examples of bone directly under the skin.

Have you ever patted your child on the head and accidently hit them lightly with a ring on? Try it on yourself. Even that hurts. Imagine a fist full of metal hitting the same spot with more force. Yeah, you're going to do some damage. If you don't know how to hit with a proper fist and just want to carry brass knuckles for self defense, even if you're just flailing around throwing your fist at everything you're bound to hit something on your attacker that will hurt him bad. That's the beauty of the brass knuckles. And on top of that they're super easy to conceal in your back pocket or purse or where ever. I keep mine in my back pocket right next to my wallet and no one is the wiser. I make sure that they're in a position I can stick my hand in my back pocket and pull it out already on my hand.

The best thing about brass knuckles are the techniques. There are no techniques. Just start wailing away. Yeah, if you're already trained in martial arts then you won't have to just swing away. You can actually target some good spots but that's not the point. That's why I said it was a great thing to carry. Because anyone can use it. Literally anyone. That is, once they learn how to actually put them on. Yes, I have shown my knuckles to people who see me putting them on the table cause when you sit down they sometimes dig into your butt. They ask about trying them on and I let them. About fifty percent of them put them on backwards or fumble around with them acting like they know how to put them on. Well that's what this chapter is for. To show you how to wear them and use them.

Once I show someone how to wear them they always say the same thing. Oh, that was easy. Then they usually do the punching air thing with them as if they've worn them all their life. Pretty easy concept.

Well that's about it. Hopefully you have got something out of reading this book. My goal was to help someone who possibly needed helping. Maybe this book was it or maybe they read this book and now have their own ideas on how to help people. Maybe you just wanted to see if there were any super secret techniques that you didn't know about because you're a black belt in something and didn't learn anything. If that's you then maybe you should write your own book.

The more people are aware of what's going on around them the better this world can be. Use the information in this book but don't let it become your life. Use it to enhance the safety of your life and that of your family.

Be happy and content with yourself and try to teach others how to do the same. If you have kids make sure you spend as much time as you can with them because before you know it they will leave and start their own life. There are no do over's and what they leave with is what you have taught them. So teach them right. And don't forget to go to the beach with them to show them how to skip rocks and find shells and sea glass. It's the little things in life that really matter.

If you're an instructor in any of the martial arts then you have to be just like a parent. Whoever you are teaching, young or old, be the example and teach them the right way. Don't make better monsters, make better people.

And above all, STFU and Be Happy............

and Aware.

ABOUT THE AUTHOR

David started his martial arts training in 1989 in Shorin-Ryu Karate at Marine Corps base Camp Hansen, Okinawa Japan with Grand Master Eizo Shimabukuro. While in the Marines, David trained in many different fighting skills including Muay Thai, Arnis, knife and gun techniques, and numerous security and intelligence oriented training and operations. Once David got out of the Marine Corps he added Isshinryu Karate, Judo, and Aikido to his training. After training at many dojo's over the years, David found his current home at Defensive Arts Dojo in Hamburg NY under Kyoshi Mike Downs and added Therien Jujitsu, Brazilian Jujitsu, and most recently Iaido into his training. David also has studied the more spiritual and intellectual aspects of martial arts including religion, Zen teachings, physics, survival, body language, micro expressions, and has been to numerous lectures and classes over all subjects.

Made in United States
North Haven, CT
09 April 2023